SHORT HOPS
AND FOUL TIPS

SHORT HOPS AND FOUL TIPS

1,734 Wild and Wacky Baseball Facts

JEFFREY LYONS AND DOUGLAS B. LYONS

TAYLOR TRADE PUBLISHING
Lanham • New York • Dallas • Boulder • Toronto • Oxford

Published by Taylor Trade Publishing
An imprint of The Rowman & Littlefield Publishing Group, Inc.
4501 Forbes Boulevard, Suite 200
Lanham, Maryland 20706

Distributed by National Book Network

Library of Congress Cataloging-in-Publication Data

Lyons, Jeffrey.
   Short hops and foul tips : 1,734 wild and wacky baseball facts / Jeffrey Lyons and Douglas B. Lyons.
      p. cm.
   ISBN 1-58979-207-6 (pbk. : alk. paper)
   1. Baseball—Miscellanea. 2. Baseball—History. I. Lyons, Douglas B. II. Title.
GV873.L86 2005
796.357—dc22   2004024023

♾™ The paper used in this publication meets the minimum requirements of American National Standard for Information Sciences—Permanence of Paper for Printed Library Materials, ANSI/NISO Z39.48–1992.
Manufactured in the United States of America.

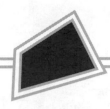

CONTENTS

I. PRELIMINARIES

II. DURING THE SEASON

III. POSTSEASON

I

PRELIMINARIES

ACKNOWLEDGMENTS

While *Short Hops and Foul Tips* is the work of the authors, we appreciate the assistance and support that has been given to us in many forms by Dan Schlossberg, Joe Castiglione, John Hagerty, Jim Ferguson, Carole Coleman, Roland A. Hemond, Bob Mayer, Dr. Fedele Vero, Dr. Eric C. Helmer of the Tampa Bay Devil Rays, Tim Phares, Marty Appel, Stephen Roney, Bob Timmerman, Clifford Otto, Eric Enders, Burt Bloom, Duke Castiglione, Bill Hickman, Rory Costello, Dave Stevens, Rod Nelson, Rim Rosenman, Peter Henrisi, Richard Thompson, Jan Castiglione, Paul Vastola, Paul Andresen, Michael DeLeo, Bragan Baldwin of the Columbus Georgia RedStixx, Phyllis Otto, David Wrzesinski of McClennan Community College, Tom Nahigian, Gary Plunkitt, Greg Beston, Jim Sandoval, Dick Bresciani of the Boston Red Sox, Jim Bouton, Chris Granozio of the New York Mets, John Speer, Clem Conley, David Perkins of the Los Angeles Dodgers, David Bruce, Wayne McElreavy, Tony Morante of the New York Yankees, Doug Pappas, Glenn Miller, Todd Fedewa and Jimmy Stanton of the Houston Astros, Bill Madden, Len Levin, Julia Patrick of Phoenix's *The Wedding Chronicle*, Andy McCue, John Matthew IV, Robert K. Fitts, PhD, Jeff and Suzie Bagwell, Dick Adams, Robert Bigelow, Carlos Diaz of the Stickball Hall of Fame, Chris Ramos of the Fresno State Media Relations Department, Charles Bevis, Steve Russell of Pennsylvania's Mid Mon Valley All Sports Hall of Fame, Jim Kaat, and Dave Smith of "Retrosheet," an invaluable research tool (www.retrosheet.org).

ACKNOWLEDGMENTS

The Society for American Baseball Research (SABR; 812 Huron Road East, Suite 719, Cleveland, Ohio 44115-1123, www.sabr.org) and its many members, research committees, and publications have always been generous with help tracking down obscure players and odd facts; Lyle Spatz, chairman of the society's research committee, Paul Howland, and Maxwell Kates rate special thanks for keeping an eye out for our kind of stories.

To our friend SABR trivia champion Scott Flatow, thanks for keeping us honest.

What is obscure to you is some SABR member's specialty. Whatever it is you want to know about baseball—no matter how arcane or obscure—there is a SABR member who knows and who is glad to share the information. Home-plate weddings? (Wait—that's *our* specialty.) Ejections? Batting champions from North Dakota? Left-handed catchers in the minor leagues? Hidden ball tricks? Somebody in SABR knows all about it and loves to talk about it.

Our friends at the National Baseball Hall of Fame continue to lend their unique and enthusiastic support to our never-ending search for the arcane, the offbeat, and the unusual. In addition to answering specific questions, they have provided us with invaluable encouragement and have always been gracious hosts during our visits to Cooperstown. Special thanks to Tim Wiles, director of research; Jeff Idelson, vice president of the Hall of Fame; Scot Mondore, manager of museum programs; Bruce Markusen, manager of program presentations; Tom Shieber, curator of new media; and James Gates Jr., the director of the Hall of Fame Library.

David Vincent, coeditor of *SABR Presents the Home Run Encyclopedia* and coauthor with Lyle Spatz and David Smith of *The Midsummer Classic: The Complete History of Baseball's All-Star Game,* is *the* expert on home runs. He has been extremely generous in helping us answer myriad home run questions. Names, dates, and unusual home run stories and statistics he has shared with us appear throughout this book. Thanks, David!

We are also grateful to Billy Bob Thornton, Bill James, Jim Kaat, Don Baylor, and Jim Bouton.

ACKNOWLEDGMENTS

We are always on the lookout for stories about home-plate weddings, ballplayers married to beauty queens, baseball license plates, unusual hobbies or off-field occupations of ballplayers, and other baseball "unusualiana." If your favorite baseball question—your stumper, the one you pull out when you meet somebody who claims to know everything about baseball—is not here, send it to us. We'll try to credit you in our next book. Contact us at Taylor Trade Publishing or email us at basbalinfo@aol.com. We'll respond.

Virtually all questions and answers in this book deal with major league baseball players of the 20th and 21st centuries. Only a few refer to 19th-century players, college players, and minor leaguers. "Modern," as used here, means post-1900. The text is up to date through the 2004 season.

DEDICATION

Douglas B. Lyons

I dedicated our first book, *Out of Left Field*, to my wife, Nancy—still my MVP. *Curveballs and Screwballs* was dedicated to our children, Susan, Margaret, Nora, and Tony.

This book is dedicated to our father, Leonard Lyons. From 1934 to 1974, LL (I never called him anything but "Pop," and I don't recall my brothers ever calling him "Dad" or "Daddy" either.) was a syndicated Broadway columnist for the *New York Post*—the old, respected and respectable *New York Post*, not the MADONNA WALKS HER DOG! DEMOCRATS STINK! SEAN PENN WITH MYSTERY WOMAN! *Post* of Rupert Murdoch.

LL was in the first graduating class at St. John's University Law School, which he attended at night, and he was a practicing lawyer. He started writing for New York's *Jewish Daily Forward* ("Hello, *Jewish Daily Forward?* I have a hot scoop—hold the back page!"), which printed an English page on Sunday. His column was called "East of Broadway." Then he started contributing short items, poems, and observations to the established columnists of the day, including Mark Hellinger, Louis Sobol, and Walter Winchell

When the *Post* held a contest to pick a new columnist, he won. Winchell named the column "The Lyons Den," and so it was—1,000 words a day, six days a week, for 40 years. Pop used to say that during his first two weeks on the job, he lost a pound a day worrying whether he'd have enough material for each day's column. The first "celebrity" he introduced himself to was Milton Berle.

LL went everywhere and knew everybody. One year, the same mail delivery brought Christmas cards from J. Edgar Hoover and Lucky Luciano. I think he's probably the only man whose correspondence file for "Lewis" included letters from Sinclair Lewis and Shari Lewis.

LL and our mother, Sylvia, were the guests of the Trumans on their last night in the White House. During dinner, Sylvia was appointed ambassador to Mexico, and LL was named a federal judge. They resigned over dessert, having served, as Pop used to say, from soup to nuts. LL's column about that occasion was nominated for the Pulitzer Prize. (He didn't win, because one of the judges said that he had been invited.)

LL introduced Y. A. Tittle to Joan Miro, and Richard Nixon to Marc Chagall. He was with Shaw on his 90th birthday. When Ernest Hemingway shot and killed himself, his widow, Mary, called LL and asked him to announce the news to the world. Pop and I were in Los Angeles at the time, and I answered the phone in our hotel room when she called.

LL always had time for my family and me. With his strange schedule, I don't know how he did it—he must have had permanent time zone fatigue—but he was at every piano recital, school play, and open school night. He was never spoiled by the famous people he knew. His favorite place to eat was at home. His favorite activity was playing baseball or football with my brothers George, Warren, and Jeffrey and me in Central Park, across the street from our Manhattan apartment. Whenever a stranger came by and asked to join us, he always said, "Sorry, it's a family game." With apologies to my good friend Eddie Feigner, LL was the greatest softball pitcher of all time: he never struck *anybody* out.

We played basketball too, in George and Warren's room. And because we lived on the 21st floor, ours was probably the highest court in the world. As the youngest, I was allowed to dunk the ball by standing on George's bed.

LL took me—and my brothers, sometimes individually and sometimes together—everywhere, always explaining, "It's part of your education." Thus, I found myself sitting next to Ernie Terrell at the last heavyweight championship fight at the old Madison Square Garden—Muhammed Ali versus Zora Foley, March 22, 1967. It was the only fight I ever went to.

We went to hundreds of Broadway shows, museums, art galleries, "happenings," bullfights, football games, and, of course, baseball games. I went with LL to Las Vegas, where he went to a newsstand in search of a New York newspaper. He returned shaking his head: "Las Vegas is the kind of town in which, when you ask for a New York newspaper, they offer you the *National Enquirer*."

One night, LL was going to see Lily St. Cyr (I think), at the time the best-known stripper in the country. I was about five, and even though I no idea what a stripper was, I didn't care. I wanted to go with him. Pop said I was too young. I didn't think so. "I am *so* old enough to see him!" I cried. Years later, he took me to see her in Lake Tahoe.

Pop must have taken me to the Polo Grounds, Yankee Stadium, and Ebbets Field, although I have no memory of any of them, except when he played in a Mayor's Trophy Game, representing the "Crumb Bums" of Toots Shor's, in a game against the "Gentlemen" of "21" at Yankee Stadium. Pop's teammates included Eddie Arcaro and Marilyn Monroe.

After Old Timers' Day, Pop often took me to the basement at Toots Shor's, where the old-timers gathered. Shor's was the original sports bar—not a place to watch the athletes on television: it's where the athletes themselves gathered. I met many ballplayers and sportswriters with Pop, but, fool that I was, I was not a baseball fan, and I recall the name of only one player I met there: Hall of Famer George "Highpockets" Kelly. I met other players with Pop—Whitey Ford, Stan Musial, Red Schoendienst, Yogi Berra, and Joe DiMaggio. I had the unique pleasure of presenting Pat Kelly, director of the photograph collection at the National Baseball Hall of Fame in Cooperstown, with two Lyons family photographs: my mother holding hands with Cy Young on his eightieth birthday—probably the best photo ever taken of either one of them; and Joe DiMaggio shaking my hand at my bar mitzvah. I suggested that Pat put the DiMaggio photo in the Hall of Fame's "Baseball/Bar Mitzvah Photos" file.

LL's column, *The Lyons Den*, appeared in over 100 newspapers all around the world. Some people occasionally refer to him as a "gossip" columnist. How he hated that word! LL was a lawyer before he became a columnist, and he prided himself on the accuracy, detail, and exclusivity of the stories he printed.

Let others write about "Which well-known Broadway actress is getting a divorce?" or "Which star is having twins?" or other such unverifiable, vindictive, blind items. LL rarely wrote a negative piece about anybody. (The exceptions were when somebody attacked him or his family or questioned his integrity.)

LL knew the great people of his generation.

Politicians: LL's copy of *Crusade in Europe* was inscribed by its author, Dwight Eisenhower, "To Leonard Lyons—a *real* writer." LL showed then–Minneapolis mayor Hubert H. Humphrey around New York's nightspots and tried to persuade him to forgo white shoes.

Athletes: At our brother George's 1961 wedding, Joe DiMaggio whispered to George, "You know, George, I gave up a doubleheader at the stadium to be here today." Said George, the most knowledgeable fan I ever met, "So did I!"

Writers: LL's friends included Hemingway (who asked LL to help him test-fire elephant guns at Abercrombie and Fitch's basement firing range), Steinbeck, Wilder, Saroyan, Michener, Capote, Vidal, Schlesinger, Kingsley, Chayefsky, Albee.

World leaders: Princess Grace, Nobel Peace Prize–winner Dr. Ralph Bunche (an annual guest, with his family, at our Seders), Chief Justices Earl Warren and Fred M. Vinson, Justice William O. Douglas, Jacob Javits, Nelson Rockefeller, John F. Kennedy.

Pop's schedule was unlike that of any other fathers I knew. He awoke at 1 PM, ate breakfast at home, and went to 10 luncheon places looking for newsworthy people. By four or so, he was at his desk at the *Post* in lower Manhattan. He was home for dinner almost every night, and after editing the next day's column with stories he had gleaned that afternoon, he stretched out on the sofa and napped until about 10 PM. He had the ability to sleep through both piano practice *and* football practice in our living room, frequently at the same time. In fact, the only thing that would wake him was our usually futile attempts to be quiet. By 11 PM, he started his evening rounds of restaurants and nightclubs, almost always starting at Sardi's, in the heart of the theatre district. By 3 or 4 AM he was home, again rewriting the next day's column. (Our mother, Sylvia, was a writer, too, and had a number of magazine articles published. Jeff and I, who shared a bedroom, could tell from the rhythm of the typewriter keys which one of our parents was typing.)[1] It's no wonder that one of my favorite songs is Leroy Andersen's "The Typewriter Song," whose sounds—the bell ringing when you approached the end of a line and the carriage return—are probably incomprehensible to today's generation. (I've been a touch typist since I was in the fourth grade and am still the fastest typist I have ever seen.) LL would call the new stories in to the *Post's* night city editor (no fax machines, no e-mails), and by 6 AM he'd be ready for bed. I used to get up at six just to spend some extra private time with him. How I loved those checker games at dawn.

DEDICATION

Shortly before the 1950 Broadway opening of *Call Me Madam*—the Irving Berlin musical about Perle Mesta, the Washington partygiver and Democratic Party fundraiser who had been named by President Truman as ambassador to Luxembourg—our parents gave a party to introduce the show's star Ethel Merman to Perle Mesta. They had never met. The party was filled with the cream of New York's theatrical and literary life, listening as Berlin sat at the piano and, with Ethel Merman, introduced such songs as "It's a Lovely Day Today" and "You're Just in Love." Joe DiMaggio—notoriously shy—stood in a corner by himself, all alone. Alone, that is, until six-year-old Jeffrey, in his pajamas, boldly walked up to him and tugged at his jacket. When DiMaggio looked at him, Jeffrey said, "Joe, you're the best guest here!"

Sorry, Jeff. You were wrong. Pop was.

Note

1. There were, of course, no word processors or computers then. But one year, my brothers and I all chipped in and, for about $125, we bought Pop an electric (not electronic) typewriter. But because the machine responded the same way no matter how hard or how lightly the individual keys were pressed, the electric typewriter homogenized the sounds of our parents typing. I think Pop would have preferred to stay with his Underwood but didn't want to hurt our feelings by telling us that.

DEDICATION

Jeffrey Lyons

This is our third book, and when it comes to dedications, nearly everyone in whose debt I will forever remain has been thanked, honored, saluted, praised, and acknowledged. But one person beyond all others is in my thoughts—my wife, Judy. For seven months a year, she somehow tolerates my Red Sox obsession; I listen to Joe Castiglione and Jerry Trupiano night and day, in the city, in the country, secretly when guests are over for dinner, during intermissions out in the street at Broadway openings on the distant Hartford, Connecticut, station. Wherever, whenever. And for reasons I will never understand, she tolerates it. Lately she's been referring to me as "this Red Sox character," mindful of the fact that wherever we go I always have some item of clothing with the Red Sox logo: a watch, a key chain, something. And yet she tolerates it . . . and me. Whenever we plan something, she will sigh and ask, "Is there a Red Sox game today?" I'd go on about all of this, but there probably *is* a Red Sox game today! Judy, my life's companion, who took great joy last October 27 when the Olde Towne Team finally won it all.

INTRODUCTION

Douglas B. Lyons

Many have asked how Jeff and I write baseball books. This is a perfectly legitimate question and has probably been asked about every pair of collaborators from Gilbert and Sullivan to Masters and Johnson. Jeff has been a baseball fan since the day he was born, although his inexplicable allegiance to the Boston Red Sox probably came a few days later.

I am not a lifelong baseball fan. In fact, I came to baseball late in life. I was 23 in 1970, when my friend Fred Koenigsberg gave me a copy of Jim Bouton's *Ball Four*. I was hooked.[1]

Since then, I have read as many baseball books as I can. I am not walking encyclopedia of baseball, although I know a few people who are. But I seem to retain the odd, the unusual, and the arcane.

I regularly read *National Sports Weekly*, *Baseball Digest*, *Baseball America*, the *New York Times*, the *New York Post*, and the *New York Daily News*. I read every team's media guide and most team yearbooks every year. I try to read the American League's Red Book and the National League's Green Book, *Who's Who in Baseball*, and the *Baseball Register*. I subscribe to many teams' online newsletters ("Astros sign three prospects!"), and I frequently read team magazines. Readers of *Out of Left Field* and *Curveballs and Screwballs,* friends, and many members of the Society for American Baseball Research generously send us items, for which we are most grateful.

Jeffrey also reads many baseball books, magazines, online columnists (with an emphasis on the Red Sox), and is adept at extracting the kind of information we like, such as that Barry Lyons and Steve Lyons (not related to us or to each other) were born the same day: June 3, 1960.

Jeff and I call or e-mail each other virtually every day to exchange items we have found. Some are ultimately deleted as too easy, too well-known, impossible to verify, a looker-upper (just a reverse record-book item), or funny but in poor taste (e.g., ballplayers who have done hard time, ballplayers who died unusual deaths, ballplayers who share names with diseases).

What we like are items that can be *confirmed* but cannot be looked up directly and that have not appeared elsewhere in this format. If a question makes us laugh, all the better.

Occasionally, we can't use an item—at least not yet—because we can't find the answer. For example: Who played in the most doubleheaders? Who broke the most bats in a career? We like to think of these as challenges, perhaps to be used in our next book.

I don't read baseball novels, and I have no interest in "fantasy" baseball. Is there a Jeffrey Maier in any fantasy league? Can a computer simulate an Earl Weaver? How about a Roger Clemens–Mike Piazza incident? How can a computer game compare to the real thing? Major League Baseball *is* my fantasy.

Also, candor dictates that I admit that I don't much care about 19th-century baseball, minor leagues or minor leaguers—unless, of course, the stories involve long or unusual names, marriages to beauty queens, dozens of children or siblings, or home-plate weddings; then, I'm interested! They're called "minor" leagues for a reason. However, I have been to a number of minor league parks—Akron, Trenton, Oneonta, Brooklyn, Dayton, Wappinger's Falls, so far—and I love the atmosphere and the prices. Plus, the games are exciting.

Major League Baseball and its 100-plus years of history—both on and off the field—are all the fantasy I need. I live near New York City and have the luxury of following both the Mets and the Yankees (and when I discuss the Yankees with Jeff, I always call them by their complete name, the "twenty-six-time World Champion New York Yankees"), so I regularly consume news of both the National and the American League.

For *Short Hops and Foul Tips*, we have created a number of new chapters and sections, such as "I Didn't Know That," "The Educated Ballplayer," and "Exactly Right."

Our next book will undoubtedly have new chapters, too. There's always more baseball.

Thank goodness!

Douglas B. Lyons

Note

1. On January 21, 2001, Jeff and I went to the annual dinner of the Baseball Assistance Team (BAT) in New York City. BAT benefits needy former ballplayers. Hundreds of players and former ballplayers were there: Shawn Green, Robin Roberts, Bill Monbouquette, George Foster, Chris Chambliss, Sandy Koufax, Dave Winfield, Tommy Lasorda, Willie Randolph, Bobby Valentine, Bill White, Pat Zachry, Bobby Thomson, Jim Palmer, and Ralph Branca, to name just a few. But for me, the thrill of the night was meeting Jim Bouton, the man who made me a fan. Although we had corresponded (if you include my sending him a six-page fan letter "corresponding"), and although he had known Jeffrey for years, we had never met. I walked right up to him, introduced myself, and uttered the single X-rated compound word that, according to *Ball Four*, was the phrase (akin to *shalom* and *aloha*) that his 1969 Seattle Pilots manager Joe Schultz used for every occasion—good, bad, or otherwise. If you want to laugh out loud or if you don't know what the word is, read *Ball Four*.

INTRODUCTION

Jeffrey Lyons

For me, baseball has always been a microcosm of life. Without getting philosophical, in my mind the baseball season is part of what makes life sweet, worth living, with all the ups and downs of the day-to-day existence we share. For a Red Sox fan, the usual triumphs of April seem like ancient history when September rolls around. But the eternal quest for a World Series flag flying over Fenway Park gets me through the long, often frigid winters in New York, and every spring hope begins again.

It was our oldest brother, George, who got me interested in baseball from the moment I came home from the hospital, it seems. He knew the history of the game better than almost anyone. One of the early collectors of baseball memorabilia, he knew obscure outfielders from the '30s, could give you the lineups of the 1916 Philadelphia Phillies, and could tell you the life story of the third-base coach of the 1952 Cincinnati Reds. Every time I see his Cardinals play, I think of him and I miss him.

Since I've become one of New York's most visible, visceral, and impassioned Red Sox fans, I constantly endure abuse, rudeness, and taunting from passersby, policemen, doormen, and even a group of obnoxious day campers last summer as I came to bat in the New York Show Business League, chanting the year the Sox last won the World Series. One day they will get theirs! I wonder where those kids are now!

My love of baseball has led to scores of friendships from those associated with the game. And this book is dedicated in part to them: Bobby Murcer, Bill White (middle name "De Kova"), and Jim Kaat are three of the finest gentlemen ever to play baseball; Bill Hands, the former Cub-Giant-Ranger-Twin hurler and my neighbor in Long Island, who never tires of my questions about his old teammates (the Sox could use a pitcher of his skills today); Ken Singleton, Michael Kay, John Sterling and Charlie Steiner often kid me in the Yankee booth, but they welcome me there as well; James Timothy McCarver, Dave Campbell, Joe Buck, Don Orsillo, and former Red Sox Jerry Remy, who always greet me when our paths cross at Fenway; "Rapid Robert" Feller, the greatest pitcher alive, who came to my bar mitzvah in 1957 (I have the photo to prove it); Dwight Evans, the Sox's best right fielder I ever saw; Frank Malzone, who deserved the Rookie of the Year in 1957 and who taught me how to pound a glove the proper way; Johnny Pesky, my favorite all-time Red Sox shortstop, who taught my daughter, Hannah, how to score a game; Yogi, who gave our father the exclusive on the infamous Copacabana fight when our father arrived moments later and at whose Museum and Learning Center I was honored to speak; and Steve Lyons, who gave me his game-worn road uniform, the one with his last name emblazoned on the back— and, of course, my favorite all-time Red Sox, who I met and interviewed only once, back in 1978, Carl Michael Yastrzemski.

This book is also for Jeff Idelson, Scot Mondore, Bill Francis, and Tim Wiles of the Baseball Hall of Fame for inviting us each year to host a movie star with a baseball connection. It is an annual thrill to visit one of the two places on Earth I consider meccas. And to Bill Kulik of the Red Sox Spanish "Béisbol" network, who lets me do color commentary with his talented announcers Uri Berenguer and J. P. Villaman. Gracias amigos! And to James Earl Jones who, though not a baseball fan, honored us with his presence at the Hall of Fame in 2004.

Joe Castiglione, the Red Sox's longtime radio voice, is like a brother; I speak with him nearly every day of my life, either on the phone or online, and his partner, Jerry Trupiano, is a superb announcer part of whose heart resides with the Cardinals. He can make stories of the Expos, Astros, and Houston Aeros (World Hockey League) sound interesting. His knack of mentioning every tiny, obscure sunbelt junior college a player may have attended for a semester or two is a delightful trademark.

But most of all I dedicate this to my family. My wife, Judy, is the most tolerant person on Earth, and those few times each season when she asks me how the Red Sox are doing or did are moments I treasure. Our children, Ben, my left fielder, and Hannah, a former catcher and my favorite equestrian competitor.

So enjoy. We're already at work on the next book!

FOREWORD

As a kid I was one of those information nuts who read every liner note of every record album. I knew the stats of every baseball and football card I had by heart. I could tell you the lineup of every team, whether they were friend or foe. A lot of that has gone by the wayside with age, but I can still tell you the lineup of the '68 Detroit Tigers who defeated my beloved Cardinals in the World Series that year.

You can't imagine my joy when Jeffrey and Douglas Lyons sent me their first book on baseball trivia and statistics. It has helped us all not only remember all those golden nuggets that faded away through the years but learn so many more that were never dreamed of. They say some bleed Dodger Blue, some Cardinal red. Well, Jeffrey and Douglas bleed the black print of every stat and anecdote ever to grace the pages of even the most obscure document about the great game that made every summer a magical wonderland of wooden bleachers, grass-stained britches, smells of hot dogs and popcorn, and the beautiful haze of a pop fly in the sun.

Jeffrey and Douglas obviously have such a deep love of America's great pastime and everything that goes into it. Let this new offering take you back to all those feelings, and while you're at it, be entertained by their intelligence and humor and their deep respect for baseball.

Billy Bob Thornton
Los Angeles, California

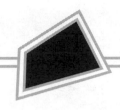

TITLE

Coming up with a title for our books is no easy matter. When we were trying to find a title for our first book, I thought of a story from 1969. That year, a man in Queens, New York, wanted to watch the New York Mets (who play in Queens) on television. His wife wanted to watch the gothic soap opera *Dark Shadows*. He kept putting on the Mets, but his wife switched the channel to *Dark Shadows*. Again, he switched it to the Mets, and she switched it right back to *Dark Shadows*. When he put the television back on to the Mets games, she tried to change the channel back to *Dark Shadows* one more time. So he killed her.

Consequently, I wanted to call the book *Turn on the Mets or I'll Kill You, and Other Stories*. But our editor would not approve.

Ok, we move on. The book had an entire chapter on home-plate weddings. Our second choice for a title was *Married at Home Plate and Other Stories*. Once again, the editor said *no*. Why? He explained, "Single men won't buy it."

So we settled on *Out of Left Field*—a baseball expression that has entered the language to mean surprising and unexpected.

For our second book, we also thought of wild, wacky titles. Jeffrey and I liked *Off the Wall*, but the editors, who were not baseball fans, did not think it was "baseball-y" enough. (I still like it.) So we settled on *Curveballs and Screwballs*.

My eight-year-old son Tony suggested a title for this book—*Rounding the Bases*—which we liked very much and had agreed upon, until another book was published with that title. Same problem with *Off the Wall*.

My next-to-last choices for a title for this book were *Harry Potter's Favourite Baseball Stories* and *Princess Diana's Favourite Baseball Stories*. They were vetoed, too.

So *Short Hops and Foul Tips* it is.

Douglas B. Lyons

II

DURING
THE
SEASON

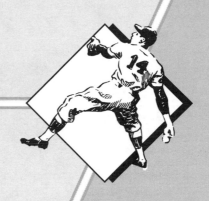

A Mound of Questions

Q Who is the first pitcher to save 40 games and win 10 games in the same season?

Billy Koch, 2002 Oakland A's: 44 saves, 11 wins.

Q "In 2003, I won the *reverse* triple crown of pitching. I led the American League in walks, wild pitches, and hit batters—only the third pitcher to win this booby prize and the first to do so in 59 years. Who am I?"

Victor Zambrano of the Tampa Bay Devil Rays: 106 walks, 115 wild pitches, and 20 hit batters.

Q Only two other pitchers have ever led their league in these three negative categories in the same season. Who are they?

George Uhle. In 1926, pitching for the Cleveland Indians, he led the American League with 118 walks, 8 wild pitches, and 13 hit batters.

Hal Gregg accomplished this dreadful triple with the 1944 Brooklyn Dodgers: 137 walks, 10 wild pitches, and 9 hit batters.

Q **Who was the first pitcher to win 20 games in a season for the New York Mets and 20 games for the Yankees?**

David Cone. He won 20 with the 1988 Mets and 20 for the 1998 Yankees.

Q **Which pitcher had the most starts in two consecutive seasons?**

Knuckleballer Wilbur Wood, Chicago White Sox: 1972, 49 starts; 1973, 48 starts. Total: 97 starts in two years.

Q **Who was the first man to do the following twice: strike out at least 200 batters in a single season while pitching for two different teams?**

Bert Blyleven. In 1976, while pitching for the Minnesota Twins and the Texas Rangers, Blyleven struck out 219 batters. In 1985, he pitched for the Cleveland Indians and the Twins, striking out a total of 206.

Q **Who is the first pitcher to win 20 games in a single season without a complete game?**

Roger Clemens, 2001 New York Yankees: 20 wins, 3 losses, no complete games.

Q **Name four pitchers who have completed seasons in which they pitched at least 70 innings and recorded ERAs of under 1.0.**

Dutch Leonard: 1914 Boston Red Sox, 224.7 innings, 0.96 ERA.
Ferdie Schupp: 1916 New York Giants, 140 innings, 0.90 ERA.
Dennis Eckersley: 1990 Oakland Athletics, 73.1 innings, 0.61 ERA.
Chris Hammond: 2002 Atlanta Braves, 76.0 innings, 0.95 ERA.

Q **Which pitcher holds the record for most consecutive innings pitched with at least one strikeout?**
Pedro Martinez of the Boston Red Sox. Between August 8 and September 10, 1999, Martinez pitched 40 consecutive innings with a least one strikeout.

Q **Whose record did Martinez break?**
His own. Between April 25 and May 23 of that same year, Martinez struck out at least one batter in 33 consecutive innings.

Q **On April 16, 2000, Chuck Finley struck out four batters in one inning—for the third time, breaking the previous record of two times. Whose record did he break?**
His own. In his first home start for Cleveland on April 16, 2000, after Luis Alicia singled for the Texas Rangers, Finley struck out Tom Evans (1), Royce Clayton (2), and Chad Curtis (3). Curtis reached base on a passed ball (K–pb). Ivan Rodriguez then singled, and Finley struck out Rafael Palmicro (4) on a 3–2 pitch.

Q **Which relief pitcher had the most career appearances without a save?**
Rich Monteleone. Pitching for the Mariners, Angels, Yankees, and Giants between 1987 and 1996, Monteleone appeared in 210 games without a save or a start.

Q **Who is the first pitcher to save 20 games one year and win 20 the next year?**
Derek Lowe, Boston Red Sox. In 2001, he saved 24 games for the Red Sox. In 2002, he became a 20-game winner, going 21–8.

Q **Many players have hit home runs in 1–0 games. Very few of them were pitchers. But only once did a Hall of Fame pitcher hit a home run off another Hall of Famer in a 1–0 game. Who were they?**

On May 5, 1965, batting for the Philadelphia Phillies, Jim Bunning homered off Warren Spahn to beat the New York Mets 1–0.

Q **Name three pitchers who won six games apiece in April.**

Vida Blue: Oakland A's, 1971.
Dave Stewart: Toronto Blue Jays, 1988.
Randy Johnson: Arizona Diamondbacks, 2000.

Q **Through 2004, only four pairs of pitching brothers have won 100 games. Who are they?**

The Perrys: Gaylord (314) and Jim (215).
The Forschs: Bob (168) and Ken (114).
The Niekros: Phil (318) and Joe (221).
The Martinezes: Pedro (182) and Ramon (135).

Q **Name five modern pitchers who have won at least 20 games in a season for three different teams.**

Grover Cleveland Alexander, Carl Mays, Joe McGinnity, Gaylord Perry, and Roger Clemens.

Q **Who was the first pitcher to win the Cy Young Award in a year which he split between the American and National Leagues?**

Rick Sutcliffe. After going 4–5 with the Cleveland Indians in 1984, he was traded to the Cubs in June. There, he went 16–1.

Q **The record book says that Rick Camp had 10 saves for the 1977 Atlanta Braves. He actually had one more. Explain.**

He helped save the life of a companion when their boat overturned in the Coosa River. Camp jumped into the freezing water to rescue his friend.

Q **On September 28, 2001, Mike Mussina recorded his 200th strikeout of the season for the New York Yankees, joining Roger Clemens at that mark. Name the last two Yankee teammates to strike out at least 200 batters in the same season.**

Jack Chesbro and Jake Powell, 1904, when the Yankees were the Highlanders. Chesbro struck out 239 and Powell 202.

Q **Only one man pitched in the majors for over 20 years but won fewer than 100 games. Who is he?**

Jesse Orosco: 24 years, 87 wins through the end of the 2004 season.

Q **How did Al Nipper prepare for his first major league start on September 6, 1983, for the Boston Red Sox?**

He read 26 books about pitching.

Q **Only four pitchers have struck out at least 2,000 batters with more strikeouts than innings pitched through 2004. Name them.**

	SO	IP
Nolan Ryan	5,714	5,386
Randy Johnson	4,161	3,368
Sandy Koufax	2,396	2,325
Pedro Martinez	2,653	2,296

Q **Who had the most career saves before throwing a no-hitter?**

Derek Lowe, Boston Red Sox. A closer for his entire career before 2002, Lowe had 85 saves with the Red Sox and briefly with the Mariners before his no-hitter at Fenway Park against the Tampa Bay Devil Rays on April 27, 2002.

Q **Who are the first three pitchers to have saved as many as 40 games in one season and thrown a no-hitter in another?**

Dennis Eckersley, Dave Righetti, and Derek Lowe.

Dennis Eckersley was an excellent starting pitcher. He threw a no-hitter for the Indians on May 13, 1977. In 1978 he went 20–8 for the Boston Red Sox. Then in 1987, after 12 years as a starter for the Indians, Red Sox, and Cubs, Eckersley became a closer for Oakland. He went on to save 390 games in his career.

After three years as an excellent starter for the New York Yankees, Dave Righetti went to the bullpen in 1984. In 1986, he saved 46 games. He pitched a no-hitter for the Yankees against the Boston Red Sox on July 4, 1983.

Derek Lowe saved 42 games for the Boston Red Sox in 2000. His no-hitter was on April 27, 2002, against the Tampa Bay Devil Rays.

Q **Who saved the most games for one team?**

Trevor Hoffman. On May 1, 2002, he recorded save #321 for the San Diego Padres. Through 2004, he had 393 career saves, including 2 for the Florida Marlins and 391 for the Padres.

Q **"I'm a Hall of Famer. I went 9 years between pitching starts. Who am I?"**

Babe Ruth. He started one game for the New York Yankees in 1921, his first year with the club, but did not start again until 1930. He walked away with wins on both of those starts. Ruth's career won–loss record is 96–46.

Q **Which pitcher went the longest—15 years!—between wins?**

Fred Johnson (1923–1938), New York Giants and St. Louis Browns.

Q **On August 26, 1991, Tom Browning of the Cincinnati Reds, who pitched a perfect game on September 16, 1988, faced Dennis Martinez, who pitched his own perfect game on July 28, 1991. This was the first time that perfect game-winners had faced each other in 25 years, since . . .**

October 2, 1966, when Sandy Koufax of the Dodgers (September 9, 1965) faced Jim Bunning of the Phillies (June 21, 1964).

TRICK QUESTION DEPARTMENT

Q **Who was the first Black to pitch a no-hitter?**

Don Black of the Cleveland Indians, July 10, 1947, a 3–0 victory over the Philadelphia A's.

Q **Name seven pitchers who won at least 20 games in a single season and who also had seasons in which they saved 20 games.**

Johnny Sain, Ellis Kinder, Jim "Mudcat" Grant, Wilbur Wood, Dennis Eckersley, John Smoltz, and Derek Lowe.

In 1946, Johnny Sain, the pride of Havana, Arkansas, won 20 games for the Boston Braves. He won 21 in 1947 and 24 in 1948. By 1954, he had moved on to the Yankees, where he saved 22 games.

Ellis "Old Folks" Kinder was a 23-game winner for the Boston Red Sox in 1949. He saved 27 games for the Sox in 1953.

Mudcat Grant won 21 games for the 1965 Minnesota Twins and saves 24 for the Oakland Athletics in 1970.

Wilbur Wood won 22, 24, 24, and 20 games for the Chicago White Sox in 1971, 1972, 1973, and 1974. He saved 20 games for the Sox in 1970.

The amazing Dennis Eckersley won 20 games for the Boston Red Sox in 1978. He went on to become the premier closer of the 1980s and 1990s: Oakland, 1988, 45 saves; 1989, 33; 1990, 48; 1991, 43; 1992, 51; 1993, 36; 1995, 29; Cardinals, 1996, 30; 1997, 36.

John Smoltz won 24 games for the 1996 Atlanta Braves. In 2002, he saved 55 games and 45 in 2003.

Derek Lowe won 21 games for the Red Sox in 2002. In 2000, he saved 42 and another 24 in 2001.

Q **Which relief pitcher recorded his 100th save in the shortest period of time?**

Kazuhiro Sasaki of the Seattle Mariners. He recorded save #100 on June 26, 2002, in a game against the Oakland A's. Sasaki made his major league debut on April 5, 2000.

Q **Only one pitcher has a career winning percentage over .700, with a minimum of 200 decisions. Who is he?**

Pedro Martinez. Through 2004, his record stands at 182–76, an incredible and record-setting winning percentage of .705.

TRICK QUESTION DEPARTMENT

Q **On April 27, 2002, Derek Lowe of the Boston Red Sox pitched a no-hitter at Fenway Park to beat the Tampa Bay Devil Rays by a score of 10–2. Who was the last pitcher before Lowe to pitch a no-hitter at Fenway Park?**

Scott Barnsby, who pitched a no-hitter for the University of Massachusetts at Fenway Park on April 22, 1997, to beat Northeastern University 1–0 in the Beanpot Baseball Tournament.

Dave Morehead was the last *major league pitcher* to throw a no-hitter at Fenway Park. He did it on September 16, 1965, before a crowd of about 2,000, a 2–0 victory over the White Sox.

Q **Which Yankee had the most consecutive starts without pitching a complete game?**

Roger Clemens. His streak of 104 starts without a complete game ran from June 3, 2000, in Atlanta through July 24, 2003, in Baltimore.

Q **Which pitcher reached 1,000 strikeouts in the fewest games?**

Kerry Wood, Chicago Cubs. By striking out Jeff Kent of the Houston Astros on August 11, 2003, Wood reached strikeout #1,000 in 134 games, improving the mark of 1,000 strikeouts in his first 143 games set by Roger Clemens.

Q **On March 31, 2004, this pitcher joined a very exclusive pitching club by becoming just the second pitcher to beat all 30 major leaguer teams. Who are the clubs' two members?**

Until that date, Al Leiter (Yankees, Blue Jays, Marlins, Mets) had been the only pitcher to beat all 30 teams. But when Kevin Brown (Rangers, Orioles, Marlins, Padres, Dodgers, Yankees), pitching for the Yankees, beat the Tampa Bay Devil Rays in Tokyo, he doubled the size of the club.

Q **Which pitcher reached 1,000 strikeouts in the fewest innings?**

Kerry Wood. His strikeout of Jeff Kent came in Wood's 853rd inning, lowering Hideo Nomo's previous record of 1,000 strikeouts in 927.2 innings.

Q **Who are the first teammates to record their 200th career wins in the same season?**

Mike Mussina and Kevin Brown, New York Yankees, 2004. Mussina's 200th win came on April 11. Brown followed with a win over the Devil Rays on April 14.

By the Numbers

.0002

Difference between first place (Albert Pujols, St. Louis Cardinals, .3587) and second place (Todd Helton, Colorado Rockies, .3585) in the race for the 2003 National League batting title.

1

Between 1950 and 1961, four men hit four home runs in a single nine-inning major league game.

Gil Hodges	August 31, 1950	Brooklyn Dodgers vs. Boston Braves
Joe Adcock	July 31, 1954	Milwaukee Braves vs. Brooklyn Dodgers
Rocky Colavito	June 10, 1959	Cleveland Indians vs. Baltimore Orioles
Willie Mays	April 10, 1961	San Francisco Giants vs. Milwaukee Braves

Q **One man was in uniform and present for all four of these incredible feats. Who was he?**
Billy Loes. In 1950 and 1954, Loes was with the Brooklyn Dodgers. By 1959, he was with the Baltimore Orioles. In 1961, Loes was a teammate of Willie Mays on the Giants.

Q **At the start of the 2002 American League Division Series between the New York Yankees and the Anaheim Angels, 22 members of the Yankees had postseason experience: Jason Giambi, Jorge Posada, Alfonso Soriano, Derek Jeter, Roger Clemens, Shane Spencer, Mariano Rivera, Mike Stanton, Bernie Williams, Randy Choate, Orlando Hernandez, Sterling Hitchcock, Steve Karsay, Ramiro Mendoza, Mike Mussina, David Wells, Chris Widger, Alex Arias, Robin Ventura, and Enrique Wilson.**
How many Angels had postseason experience?
Only one: Kevin Appier. In 2000, he pitched two games in the American League Division Series for the Oakland A's.

Q **On, May 24, 1947, Carl Furillo of the Brooklyn Dodgers did something in a home game against the Philadelphia Phillies that no ballplayer had ever done before—or since. What did he do?**
Batting for Gene Hermanski, he hit a pinch-hit home run *in the first inning*.

1.2

Q **As of 2004, which is the only major league team to conduct spring training in its home city?**

The Tampa Bay Devil Rays. Their spring training park, Progress Energy Park (Al Lang Field) in St. Petersburg, Florida, is just 1.2 miles from Tropicana Stadium.

Before the Devil Rays, the last time teams trained in their home city was in 1919, when the St. Louis Cardinals and the Philadelphia Athletics trained at home.

In addition to the Devil Rays, Al Lang Field has been the spring home of many teams since 1916, including the Phillies, Indians, Yankees, Dodgers, and Cardinals.

2

Q **Who are the only two men to give up homers to both Lou Gehrig and Mickey Mantle?**

Randy Gumpert and Bob Feller.

Q **Only two New York Yankees have hit 30 home runs and stolen 30 bases in the same season. On August 17, 2002, Alfonso Soriano became the second (and the first second baseman) to accomplish this feat. Who was the first?**

Bobby Bonds, in his only year with the Yankees, 1975: 32 home runs, 30 stolen bases.

ADDS NEW MEANING TO THE WORD SLUG-GER DEPARTMENT

Q **How many players can you name who have played with two bullets in them?**

Pitcher Nick Bierbrodt: Tampa Bay Devil Rays, Boston Red Sox. He was shot on June 7, 2002, in Charleston, South Carolina, where he was on a rehab assignment. Two slugs are still in his liver.

Q **Only twice in major league history have two players with the same name homered in the same game. Who are they?**

The first two were George Kenneth Griffey (Sr. and Jr.) for the Seattle Mariners on September 14, 1990. (It helped that they were the first father-and-son teammates.)

Q **When was the second time that two men with the same name homered in the same game?**

It happened on April 7, 2004, when Luis Gonzalez homered for the Arizona Diamondbacks. Luis Gonzalez also homered for the Colorado Rockies.

Too bad boxer George Forman and his four sons—George, George, George, and George—didn't play baseball.

Q **Only two Canadians have played for both the Expos and the Blue Jays. Who are they?** Hint: One is a native of Toronto, and the other is from Montreal.

Toronto native Rob Ducey: Blue Jays, 1987–1992, 2000; Expos, 2001.
Montreal native Denis Boucher: Blue Jays, 1991; Expos, 1993–1994.

3

Q **Who are the first three men to have consecutive seasons in which they hit 35 home runs and stole 35 bases?**

	Team	HR	SB
Willie Mays	1956 NY Giants	36	40
	1957 NY Giants	35	38
Barry Bonds	1996 SF Giants	42	40
	1997 SF Giants	40	37
Alfonso Soriano	2002 Yankees	39	41
	2003 Yankees	38	35

Q **Only three sets of brothers have been teammates on three different teams since 1900. Who are they?**
Lloyd and Paul Waner were teammates with the Pittsburgh Pirates from 1927 to 1940, the Boston Braves briefly in 1941, and the Brooklyn Dodgers in 1944.

Bobby and Billy Shantz. Wilmer Ebert "Billy" Shantz was in the majors for only parts of three seasons. In 1954, he played in 51 games for the Philadelphia Athletics. In 1955, he appeared in just 79 games for the Kansas City Athletics. He did not play again in the majors until 1960, when he appeared in one game (with no at bats) for the New York Yankees. In each of those seasons, his brother Bobby was a teammate.

Roberto Alomar and Sandy Alomar Jr. The sons of Sandy Alomar Sr. were teammates on the San Diego Padres, 1988–1989. They reunited on the Cleveland Indians, 1999–2000, and on the Chicago White Sox in 2003.

4

Q **Only four men have been ejected from major league games in six different decades. Which four?**
Casey Stengel, Leo Durocher, Frank Robinson, and Don Zimmer.
Thanks to Doug Pappas, the *ejection expert, for this unusual record.*

Q **Who are the first four men to hit .300 with 100 runs scored and 40 stolen bases in their rookie seasons?** Hint: None is a Hall of Famer—yet.

	Team	BA	R	SB
Jimmy Barrett	1900 Cincinnati Reds	.316	114	44
Joe Jackson	1911 Cleveland Indians	.408	126	41
Ichiro Suzuki	2001 Seattle Mariners	.350	127	56
Scott Podsednik	2003 Milwaukee Brewers	.314	100	43

5

In the early years of the major leagues, one umpire was the rule. Starting in 1898, two umpires were assigned to major league games.

The majors went to three umps per game in the 1920s and 1930s when reserve umpires worked important games. Three-man crews became regular in 1933.

Four umpires became the norm in 1952, although they were used for part of the 1909 World Series and in the subsequent Series through 1946.

The first World Series with a six-man crew was in 1947.

Q **How many umpires worked the very last game ever played at Ebbets Field, Pirates vs. Dodgers, September 27, 1957?**

Five. Rookie umpire Ed Sudol gained valuable on-the-field experience working with Augie Donatelli, Vic Delmore, Vinnie Smith, and future Hall of Famer Jocko Conlon.

Sudol went on to a 20-year career in the National League.

Q **Who are the first five Red Sox players to hit at least 20 home runs in each of their first four major league seasons?**

Ted Williams, Tony Conigliaro, Jim Rice, Nomar Garciaparra, and Brian Daubach.

Q **Who are the only five men to homer in November?**

The 2001 baseball season took a one-week hiatus after the tragedies of September 11, pushing the playoffs back a week. The Diamondbacks–Yankees World Series didn't start until October 27.

Game 4 of the Series started on October 31, but by the time Derek Jeter came to bat in the 10th inning, it was after midnight—November 1, 2001. The Yankee Stadium message board flashed, ATTENTION FANS: WELCOME TO NOVEMBER BASEBALL! Jeter's walk-off home run was the first ever in November.

In Game 5, which started somewhat later on November 1, home runs were hit by Steve Finley and Rod Barajas of the Arizona Diamondbacks and by Scott Brosius of the Yankees.
Alfonso Soriano homered the latest ever, in Game 7 on November 4.

6

Joe Magrane started playing high school baseball when he was still in the seventh grade. He earned six high school letters in baseball.

7

Number of protective cups broken during his career by Johnny Bench.

8

Q **Which player has the most-swelled head?**

Kevin Mench, Texas Rangers. Like manager Bruce Bochy, Mench wears a size 8 hat.

12

Jerry Mumphrey was awarded 12 high school letters in baseball, football, and basketball.

29

The San Diego Padres had just 29 sacrifices in 2001, the fewest in the history of the National League.

9,399,999.99

On December 2, 2000, Turk Wendell signed a three-year contract with the New York Mets. With incentives, it was worth $9,399,999.99 over three years—just one cent short of $9.4 million. Wendell's signing bonus was $299,999.99. Wendell wore #99 with the Mets.

Extra Innings

EXACTLY RIGHT!

Jim Kaat: 16 Gold Gloves, 16 home runs.

Casey Stengel wore #37 and won 37 World Series games.

Charlie Hough: 216 career wins, 216 career losses.

Stan Musial: 1,815 hits on the road, 1,815 hits at home (of course, he had many more at bats at home than on the road).

Warren Spahn: 363 wins, 363 base hits.

BASEBALL GIVETH, BASEBALL TAKETH AWAY DEPARTMENT

Q **On July 26, 2000, Rob Ducey was traded from the Phillies to Toronto. He moved out of his apartment and left town. What happened to him 10 days later?**

He was traded back to the Phillies.

Q **Name a big leaguer who is a former President.**

Enrique Burgos. Before breaking in to the majors in 1993 with the Kansas City Royals, he pitched for the President Lions in the Taiwan Professional Baseball League.

Q **Name a team that broadcasts all of its games in Wales.**

Boston Red Sox. Wales, Massachusetts, is about 60 miles southwest of Boston.

Q **Which team broadcasts all of its games in Lima and throughout Peru?**

Cincinnati Reds. You can hear them on WIMA in Lima, Ohio, and WARU in Peru, Indiana.

Q **What did Bob Feller do exactly sixty years after he threw a no-hitter on Opening Day, April 16, 1940, for the Cleveland Indians?**

He threw out the ceremonial first pitch at Jacobs Field, new home of the Indians, April 16, 2000.

There must be a special yin–yang place in the record books for Rickey Henderson. Through 2004, he holds the following reciprocal records:

Most stolen bases in a career, 1,406; most times caught stealing in a career, 335.

Most stolen bases in a season, 130; most times caught stealing in a season, 42.

Most stolen bases in a career in the American League, 1,307; most times caught stealing in a career in the American League, 293.

Close to Henderson on the yin–yang scale are Cy Young (most career wins, 511; most career losses, 316) and Nolan Ryan (most career strikeouts, 5,714; most career walks surrendered, 2,795).

THE ALL-HOUSE TEAM

Tom House, Phil Roof, Matt Stairs, Darren Hall, Gene Alley, Rolando Roomes, Paul Householder, coach Ron Plaza, Vallie Eaves.

Q **Only one team has a souvenir store outside the United States and Canada. Which team and where is it?**
San Diego Padres. The store is in Tijuana, Mexico.

Q **Eddie Gaedel is the only major leaguer who was a midget. He stood 3'7". Name a major leaguer who was a Midget.**
Rob Ducey. Before becoming a major league baseball player, he played for the Canadian National Midget Softball Team.

Q **Chris Chambliss's favorite food is swordfish. Which delicacy is fancied by Julio Machado (Mets, Brewers, 1989–1991)?**
Iguana.

Q **Was September 9, 2003, a good day for Justin Duchscherer?**
Yes and yes.
   1. He made his debut with the Oakland A's.
   2. His first child Evan Jacob was born.

UNDER NEW MANAGEMENT

Q **One of baseball's oldest clichés (and as Steve Allen might have asked, how come there are no new clichés?) is that a manager is "hired to be fired." Most are—eventually. Most, but not all. How many men can you name who managed in the big leagues for at least eight years and were never fired?**
Hint: Not Connie Mack. He was fired as manager of the Pittsburgh Pirates in 1896.

Walter Alston retired in 1976, after 23 years as the Dodgers' manager.

Ralph Houk resigned from the Yankees in 1963 to become general manager; he resigned from the Yankees in 1973; he retired from the Tigers in 1978; and he retired from the Red Sox in 1984 after managing for 20 years.

Dick Howser resigned from the Yankees in 1980. After eight years as a big league manager, he retired from the Royals in 1986 due to ill health.

Tommy Lasorda retired from the Dodgers in 1996 after 21 years at the helm.

Jim Leyland resigned from the Pirates in 1996, from the Marlins in 1998, and from the Rockies in 1999 after a 14-year major league managerial career.

Danny Murtaugh resigned from the Pirates in 1964, 1967, 1971, and 1976, all for health reasons. He managed in the majors for 15 years.

Tom Kelly's only managerial job was as skipper of the Minnesota Twins. He retired after managing the Twins for 16 years, 1987–2001.

Thanks to Maxwell Kates for contributing this odd list.

There may be no crying in baseball, as Tom Hanks said in *A League of Their Own*, but in games pitched by Joe Horlen (who played as Joel: White Sox, A's, 1961–1972), there were tissues.

He was ahead of his time. Instead of chewing tobacco, he chewed wads of tissue.

Before every start, pitcher Carl Morton (Expos, Braves, 1969–1976) read a book about psychocybernetics.

TRICK QUESTION DEPARTMENT

Q How did the 2002 All-Star game end?
Hint: Not in a tie.

The Frontier League All-Star Game was tied at 7 after 11 innings at Homer Stryker Field in Kalamazoo, Michigan, on July 10, 2002. The game pitted the All-Stars of the East against those of the West. The Major League All-Star game, played the day before, had ended in an unsatisfying tie when both teams ran out of pitchers.

So a home run derby was held in Kalamazoo to decide the winner. Three batters from each team got five pitches apiece. Most home runs wins. Brody Jackson's two homers put the West on top, 2–1.

Q Only once in the history of no-hitters has a Hall of Fame fielder recorded the last out of a game, catching a ball hit by a Hall of Fame batter to preserve a no-hitter pitched by a Hall of Famer. Name all three.
On July 20, 1958, Ted Williams of the Boston Red Sox flied to right fielder Al Kaline of the Detroit Tigers and became the final victim of Jim Bunning's no-hitter.

THE FALL CLASSIC

Q **When was the first World Series played entirely west of the Mississippi?**

The World Series of 1944, which pitted the St. Louis Cardinals against the St. Louis Browns (their only appearance in the Fall Classic.) All six games were played at Sportsmans Park, the stadium that both teams shared just west of the Mississippi.

The Cardinals won the "Streetcar Series" 4–2.

Q **Who was the first man to hit World Series home runs at both Shea Stadium and Yankee Stadium?**

Mike Piazza, New York Mets. On October 22, he homered in Game 2 of the 2000 World Series, in a 6–5 loss to the Yankees at Yankee Stadium.

On October 25, in Game 4 at Shea Stadium, Piazza homered again, in a 4–2 Mets victory, but the Yankees went on to win the Series, 4 games to 1.

Q **Who went the longest between World Series appearances?**

Jim Kaat—17 years. His first appearance in the Series was in 1965 with the Minnesota Twins. He won Game 2 and lost Games 5 and 7 as the Twins lost the Series to the Los Angeles Dodgers 4–3. He didn't return to the Series until 1982, with the St. Louis Cardinals. Kaat had no decision in Games 1, 2, 3, and 4 as the Cardinals beat the Milwaukee Brewers 4–3.

Q **Name a man—perhaps the only man—who turned down a legitimately earned World Series ring**.
Frank Crosetti. During his playing career with the New York Yankees (1932–1948), "Crow" played on World
Championship teams in 1932, 1936, 1937, 1938, 1939, 1941, and 1943. He then coached for the Yankees, mostly
at third base, 1947–1968, helping the Yankees win the Series in 1950, 1951, 1952, 1953, 1956, 1958, 1961, and
1962. Not to sell Crosetti short, in 1942, 1955, 1957, 1960, 1963, and 1964, his Yankees lost the World Series but
were the American League champions.

In 1962, Crosetti decided that he had enough World Championship rings and asked the Yankees for something instead: a set of shotguns.

Frank Crosetti told us in 2001 that he still had the shotguns, emblazoned with the Yankees logo. Here's what
he said:

*Now that I look back, I should have gotten more rings. This way, I would have had rings for my grandchil-
dren (three) and great-grandchildren (two, so far). My wife has one, I have two, and my daughter and son have
one each.*

*The first gun I received for a World Series win was a Winchester 20-gauge pump gun, 26-inch barrel, with
matted rib and beavertail forearm. On the right side was the inscription "Presented to Frank Crosetti by the
Baseball Commissioner as a member of the New York Yankees World Champions, 1939."*

*In 1950 I received a Browning 20-gauge over-and-under, 26-inch barrels. But Frick made me put a round
sterling silver emblem on the stock—a Yankee emblem with "World Champions, 1950" at the top and my name
at the bottom.*

*Then, I believe, the following year I received another 20-gauge Browning over-and-under with different bar-
rel borings. I did not have to put a Yankee emblem on this one.*

*Then, maybe the same year, I received a 28-gauge automatic Remington with 26-inch ventilated rib barrel—
nothing on the stock.*

Q **Denny McClain of the Detroit Tigers was scheduled to pitch on October 2, the first game of the 1968 World Series for the Detroit Tigers, facing Bob Gibson of the St. Louis Cardinals in St. Louis. Although McClain was a true competitor, he was also loose before the game. What did he play to stay loose?**

"Stardust" as well as some rock-and-roll songs. McClain played an organ in a lounge off the hotel lobby where the Tigers were staying. McClain and the Tigers lost that first game.

Q **The 1969 Mets have become legendary—winning the World Series in only their seventh year of existence over the heavily favored Baltimore Orioles. Only one member of the 1969 Mets had been in a World Series before 1969. Who is he?**

Ron Taylor. He pitched in Games 4 and 6 of the 1964 World Series for the St. Louis Cardinals, who beat the Yankees 4 games to 3. In the 1969 Series, Taylor (later Ron Taylor, M.D.) pitched in Games 1 and 2.

FIRST OF ALL

Q **No American closer has saved 50 games in two seasons. Why not?**

Because the first man to save 50 games in two seasons is Eric Gagne of the Los Angeles Dodgers. He saved 52 games in 2002 and 55 in 2003. Gagne is a native of Montreal, Quebec, Canada.

Q **Who is the first man to hit three home runs on his birthday?**

Nomar Garciaparra, Boston Red Sox, July 23, 2002. Happy 29th birthday!

Q **Who is the first player in the history of the National League to drive in at least 100 runs for 9 consecutive seasons?**

Sammy Sosa, Chicago Cubs, 1995–2003.

Q **When was the first time that two teams engaged in a clash over jewelry?**

On August 25, 2001, the Indians were playing in Seattle. Arthur Rhodes came on to pitch for the Mariners in the ninth inning, as Omar Vizquel stepped up to the plate. Vizquel complained to the umpires that the glare from Rhodes's earrings was distracting. Rhodes was ordered to remove the earrings, which he had worn for two years without complaint. The earrings, worth about $10,000 each, represented Rhodes's two daughters. He resisted, and both benches emptied. No punches were thrown, but a shouting match ensued. Eventually, Rhodes removed the earrings, but he was also removed from the game.

Ever graceful, Rhodes later referred to the 5'9" Vizquel as "a little midget."

Q **During the 2003 season, pitcher Dan Miceli did something that no other pitcher had ever done. What did he do?**

He pitched in four different divisions. He started the season with the Colorado Rockies in the National League West. Then he went to the Houston Astros in the National League Central.

Next, it was off to the New York Yankees in the American League East. His last stop in 2003 was with the Cleveland Indians in the American League Central.

Q **Who was the first man to pitch more than 250 innings in his career and allow more walks than hits?**

Mitch Williams. During his 11-year career with the Rangers, Cubs, Phillies, Astros, Angels, and Royals, Williams pitched 691.3 innings, surrendering 544 walks and 537 hits.

Q **Who was the first man to pitch for the Yankees, the Mets, and the Astros?**

Dwight Gooden: Mets (1984–1994), Yankees (1996–1997, 2000), Astros (2000). "Dr. K" also pitched for the Indians (1998–1999) and the Devil Rays (2000).

Q **Who was the first broadcaster to interview the president of the United States at a baseball game?**

Vince Lloyd, April 10, 1961, at Griffith Stadium in Washington, D.C., home of the Senators. The president was John F. Kennedy. Lloyd was a broadcaster for the Chicago White Sox.

Q **Who was the first man to do the following *twice*: hit 20 homers in a season while splitting the season between both leagues.**

Glenallen Hill. In 1998, he hit 12 homers for the Mariners, then 8 after his trade to the Cubs. In 2000, he hit 11 home runs with the Cubs and another 16 with the Yankees.

Q **Who was the first big leaguer to wear a "Catcher-Cam" television camera attached to his mask?**

Brad Ausmus, Houston Astros, August 12, 1997.

Q **Who was the first manager to hold the career win record for two different teams?**

George "Sparky" Anderson. During his tenure as the Cincinnati Reds manager, 1970–1978, his team won 863 games. From 1979 to 1995, he managed the Detroit Tigers, winning 1,331 games.

Q **Who is the first shortstop to record 2,000 career hits, 170 home runs, and 350 steals?**

Barry Larkin, Cincinnati Reds.

Q **Name the first team to finish in last place while leading the league in home attendance.**

The 1999 Colorado Rockies. Home attendance at Coors Field was 3,481,065, but the team finished last in the National League, 28 games out of first place.

Q **When was the first time in the majors that two Japanese-born starting pitchers faced each other?**

May 7, 1999, when Hideki Irabu of the New York Yankees beat Mac Suzuki of the Seattle Mariners 10–1.

On June 18, 1997, Hideo Nomo of the Dodgers and Shigetoshi Hasegawa of the Angels appeared in the same game. Neither figured in the decision.

Q **Who was the first manager in the National League to guide his team to at least 90 wins in his first five seasons?**

Davey Johnson of the New York Mets. In 1984, the Mets were 90–72. In 1985, they 98–64, and in 1986, their record was 108–54, as the Mets beat the Boston Red Sox to win the World Series. In 1987, the Mets' record was 92–70, and in 1988, Johnson guided the Mets to a record of 100–60, best in the National League East.

Q **Which was the first team with its own website?**

Seattle Mariners: www.mariners.org went online November 30, 1994.

Q **Who was the first man to hit three home runs in a game three times *in the same season*?**

Sammy Sosa. He had his third three-homer game of the 2001 season on September 23, 2001, in Houston. His homers were number 56, 57, and 58 for the season.

Q **Who were the first teammates to hit three home runs each in the same game?**

Jeromy Burnitz and Richie Sexson of the Milwaukee Brewers. They helped their team defeat the Arizona Diamondbacks 9–4 in Phoenix on September 25, 2001.

Q **Who is the first player in big league history to smack at least 100 extra-base hits in two consecutive seasons?**

Todd Helton of the Colorado Rockies: 2000, 103; 2001, 105.

Q **Who were the first African Americans to be on a World Series winner?**

Larry Doby and Satchel Paige, 1948 Cleveland Indians.

Q **Who was the first African American to play for Boston?**
Sam Jethroe. He made his debut with the Boston Braves on April 18, 1950.

Q **A number of ballplayers have homered in their first major league at bats. Who was the first to do so against a "reigning" Cy Young Award winner?**
Marcus Thames, New York Yankees, off Randy Johnson of the Arizona Diamondbacks, June 10, 2002.

Q **Who was the first outfielder to have 10 putouts in a game twice in one season?**
Roy Weatherly, New York Yankees.

Q **Who is the first player to collect 400 total bases in consecutive seasons?**
Todd Helton, Colorado Rockies: 2000, 405 bases; 2001, 402 bases.

Q **Name the first National League team to sweep an entire season series from another National League team?**
By beating the Colorado Rockies on October 3, 2002, the Atlanta Braves completed the first season sweep in the league's history, winning all 13 games against Colorado.

Q It happened on June 18, 2002, when the Texas Rangers visited the Chicago Cubs. It never happened before. What was it?

The game brought together four players each of whom had hit 400 home runs. The Cubs featured Sammy Sosa (475) and Fred McGriff (459). The Rangers included Rafael Palmeiro (460, including one that night) and Juan Gonzalez (401). Total home runs by these four as of that day: 1,795. The Cubs beat the Rangers 4–3. The lineup cards were sent to the Hall of Fame.

Q When was the first time that managers from the Dominican Republic faced each other?

On June 25, 2002, Tony Peña of the Royals faced Luis Pujols of the Detroit Tigers in Kansas City. Hipolito Mejia, president of the Dominican Republic, was present for the game.

Q Who is the first second baseman to drive in 100 runs six years in a row?

Jeff Kent, San Francisco Giants, 1997–2002.

Q Who is the first American umpire to work home plate for a Japanese All-Star game?

Jim Evans, a native of Longview, Texas. He called balls and strikes during the game in Fukuoka in 1991.

TRICK QUESTION DEPARTMENT

Q **Who is the first graduate of the Massachusetts Institute of Technology (MIT, home of the Engineers) to play in the major leaguers?**

Jason Szuminski of the San Diego Padres, who graduated from MIT in 2000 with a degree in aeronautical engineering. Szuminski is the first engineer to play in the majors after *finishing* MIT.

Q **But two other men went to MIT *after* their major league playing days were over. Who are they?**

Skip Lockwood. After a 12-year major league career (1965–1980) with the Seattle Pilots, Milwaukee Brewers, California Angels, New York Mets, and Boston Red Sox, Lockwood got an SM degree from MIT in 1983.

The other ballplayer with a degree from MIT is Art Merewether, MIT class of 1925. Before that, he had one at-bat for the Pittsburgh Pirates on July 10, 1922. Merewether became the president of the American Meteorological Society.

Q **When was the first time that a pitcher with over 300 wins to his credit faced a batter with over 600 home runs?**

April 7, 2004, when Roger Clemens of the Houston Astros (310 career wins) faced Barry Bonds of the San Francisco Giants in Houston. Bonds had 659 home runs at the time but did not homer off Clemens.

Q **Who is the first Yankee starting pitcher to make his Yankee debut in a home opener?**

Javier Vasquez, April 8, 2004. He pitched 7 strong innings, giving up just one run, as the Yankees beat the White Sox 3–1.

HIGHS AND LOWS

Q **Who had the most hits in April?**

Darin Erstad of the Anaheim Angels. In April 2000, he had 48 hits.

Q **Who hit the most home runs at a single away ballpark?**

Willie Mays. He hit 54 home runs at Chicago's Wrigley Field.

Q **Who had the most home runs in a season before being traded in the month of June?**

David Justice had 21 home runs for the Cleveland Indians before his trade to the Yankees on June 29, 2000. He hit another 20 for New York in their drive to the World Series.

Q **Which pitcher won the most games at a single ballpark since 1920?**

Steve Carlton. He won 138 games at Philadelphia's Veterans Stadium.

Q **Who hit the most career home runs on his birthday?**

Al Simmons, who hit five homers on his birthday, May 22. Among those who hit four homers on their birthdays are Hall of Famers Lou Gehrig, Joe Morgan, Tony Perez, Duke Snider, José Canseco, Kirk Gibson, Lance Parrish, Jason Thompson, and Gus Zernial.

Thanks to David Vincent for this one.

Q **Which opposing player has played the most games against the Yankees at Yankee Stadium?**

Cal Ripken Jr. His final game at Yankee Stadium, on September 30, 2001, was his 126th game at the Stadium—the most by any opposing player.

Q **St. Louis's Busch Stadium opened on May 12, 1966. The Cardinals have played there ever since— 38 years of Redbird baseball. Mark McGwire was traded from the Oakland A's to the Cardinals on July 31, 1997, and it only took him until June 30, 2000, to set the record for most career home runs at Busch Stadium. On that date, he hit career home run #105 at Busch. Whose record did he break?**

Ray Lankford—a Cardinal since 1990.

Q **Which team has had the longest road trip?**

The top two answers:

The 1992 Houston Astros. To make room for the Republican National Convention at the Astrodome, the Astros embarked on a 26-game, 28-day road trip, which covered 9,186 miles from July 27 to August 23. Their itinerary: Atlanta, Cincinnati, Los Angeles, San Diego, San Francisco, Chicago, St. Louis, Philadelphia.

In 1944, the Philadelphia Phillies played more games (28) in fewer days (27), August 4–30. They finished that season at 61–92, dead last in the National League.

In 1994, when ceiling tiles at the Kingdome fell during the regular season, the Seattle Mariners embarked on a road trip between July 22 (in Boston) and August 11.

Q **Which Hall of Famer had the most at-bats in a single season without hitting a home run?**
Hint: Not Rod Carew. True, in 1972 Carew led the American League in batting (.318) without a single homer, but that was in only 535 at bats.

In 1922, Rabbit Maranville came to bat 672 times for the Pittsburgh Pirates, hitting .295, but had no homers.

Q **"I played in only 88 games in the majors. Nevertheless, I played for five different teams, the post-1925 record for most teams in the fewest games. Who am I?"**
Joe Morgan, best known as the manager of the Boston Red Sox, 1988–1991. He played for the Milwaukee Braves (13 games), Kansas City Athletics (20 games), Cleveland Indians (26 games), Philadelphia Phillies (26 games), and St. Louis Cardinals (3 games).

Thanks to Joe Morgan himself, who gave us this odd question in Fort Myers, Florida, during spring training 2002.

Q **Who is the tallest player in the history of the game? How tall is he?** Hint: Not Randy Johnson.
Jon Rauch, pitcher, 2002 Chicago White Sox. 6'11".

Q **Who has hit home runs for the most teams since 1900?**
Todd Zeile. His home run for the New York Yankees on April 2, 2003, marked the 10th major league team for which he had homered. Zeile hit 5 for the Expos. The others are the Cardinals, Cubs, Orioles, Phillies, Dodgers, Rangers, Marlins, Mets, and Rockies.

Q **Which pitcher has won the most games after "Tommy John" surgery?**

Through the 2004 season, David Wells had recorded 212 wins after reconstructive surgery for a torn elbow ligament—colloquially known as "Tommy John" surgery.

Q **Which first-round draft pick spent the most time in the minor leagues before making his big league debut?**

Alan Zinter. He was the 24th pick in the first round of the 1989 draft by the New York Mets and spent the next 13 years in the minors. He made his major league debut with the Houston Astros on June 18, 2002.

Q **Coors Field in Denver, home of the Rockies, is the highest of the 30 major league ballparks, at 5,280 feet above sea level. Which is the lowest?**

San Francisco's SBC Park, home of the Giants. It is exactly at sea level, right on San Francisco Bay.

Q **Which player on a World Championship team led his team with the fewest RBIs?**

Larry Gardner of the 1916 Boston Red Sox. He led the team with a grand total of 62 RBIs.

Q **Which pitcher who wore glasses won the most games?**

Orel Hershiser? No. He won 204 games. Good guess.

Greg Maddux? Another good guess, but also wrong. Maddux won 210 games before LASIK eye surgery on July 10, 1999—after which he did not wear glasses. By the way, Maddux pitched and won again on July 11, the day after his eye surgery.

The answer is Mel Harder, who won 223 games for the Cleveland Indians between 1928 and 1947.

IT'S A HIT!

499–500–501

Q **Who is the only man to hit home runs #499 and #500 in the same game?**
Frank Robinson, Baltimore Orioles, September 13, 1971.

Q **What's the connection: Babe Ruth, Willie Mays, Mark McGwire, Mike Schmidt, Ted Williams, Mel Ott.**
They hit home runs #499 and #500 on successive days.

Q **Only one man who hit 500 career home runs never led his league in home runs in any single season. Who is he?**
Rafael Palmeiro.

Q **How many players have collected at least 100 hits in each of their first 20 years in the major leagues?**
Only two.
Carl Yastrzemski, Boston Red Sox, 1961–1980.
Eddie Murray, Baltimore Orioles, New York Mets, Los Angeles Dodgers, Cleveland Indians; 1977–1996.

Q **Who went the longest between home runs #499 and #500?**

Sammy Sosa. He hit #499 on September 29, 2002, but had to wait 187 days before hitting #500, on April 4, 2003.

Q **Only two members of the 500–home run club hit #500 and #501 in the same game. Who are they?**

Harmon Killebrew (August 10, 1971) and Mark McGwire (August 15, 1999).

Q **Who went the longest between home runs #500 and #501?**

Jimmie Foxx. He hit #500 on September 24, 1940; #501 didn't come until April 25, 1941, 10 games into the 1941 season, 17 games and 213 days later.

Q **Who was the first future Hall of Famer to surrender a home run to Mickey Mantle?**

Satchel Paige. On August 29, 1951, Mantle took Paige deep, as the Yankees beat the St. Louis Browns 15–2. The homer was the ninth of Mantle's career

WHY DID THE MARLINS FINISH 15 GAMES OUT OF FIRST PLACE IN 2000? DEPARTMENT

Q **Luis Castillo of the Florida Marlins had a good year in 2000—180 hits and a .334 batting average. How many runs did he drive in?**

17.

Q **In 1996, Vinny Castilla hit 40 home runs and drove in 113 runs for the Colorado Rockies. How did he do in 1997?**

About the same—40 home runs and 113 RBIs.

Q **The first two batters in a game have homered on a number of occasions. These two players led off games with home runs three times—including twice in one season Who are they?**

Pete Rose and Bobby Tolan both homered to lead off for the Reds on April 7 and August 17, 1969, and on June 28, 1970.

Q **On April 13, 1987, for the first time in big league history, the first *three* batters all homered. Who were they?**

Marvell Wynne, Tony Gwynn, and John Kruk of the San Diego Padres. The hard-luck pitcher for the San Francisco Giants who gave up these three homers was Roger Mason.

Between 1901 and 1960, the American League had eight teams. During those years, only three men had single seasons in which they hit at least two home runs in each park in the league. They were Babe Ruth (1921, then four consecutive years, 1926, 1927, 1928, and 1929—one of Ruth's monumental but frequently overlooked accomplishments), Jimmie Foxx (1932), and Joe DiMaggio (1937).

Between 1961 and 1968, the American League had 10 teams. During those years, only Mickey Mantle (1961) and Harmon Killebrew (1962) hit multiple homers in every city in a single season.

The National League had eight teams from 1901 to 1960. The men who hit multiple homers in each league city in a single season during those years are Del Ennis (1948), Ralph Kiner (1949), Sid Gordon (1950), Gil Hodges (1952), Eddie Mathews (1953 and 1959), Willie Mays (1955), Hank Aaron (1958), and Orlando Cepeda (1961).

Nobody hit multiple homers in each of the 10 National League cities in a single season during the seven years there were 10 cities in the National League, 1962–1968.

Thanks to David Vincent for this analysis.

Q **Sure, Jimmie Foxx celebrated on September 24, 1940. In the sixth inning of the first game of a doubleheader at Shibe Park against the Philadelphia A's, he, Ted Williams, Joe Cronin, and Jim Tabor all hit home runs for the Boston Red Sox—the first time in the history of the American League that four batters had homered in the same inning. Why else was Foxx celebrating?**
Jimmie Foxx's home run was his 500th.

Q **Who are the only two men to hit leadoff homers in both games of a doubleheader?**
Harry Hooper and Rickey Henderson.

Q **What's the connection: Jerry Koosman and Joe McEwing.**
Both were traded for Jesse Orosco 22 years apart. Koosman was traded by the Mets to the Twins for Jesse Orosco in December 1978. On March 18, 2000, the Mets traded Orosco to the Cardinals for Joe McEwing.

Q **Who are the only men to hit 500 home runs and have a W?**
Babe Ruth and Jimmie Foxx.
   Ruth was a great pitcher before he became a full-time outfielder. His pitching record was 94–46, with an ERA of 2.28. He hit 714 home runs.
   Foxx pitched in two games and earned a victory in 1945 for the Phillies. He hit 534 home runs.

Q **What did Jorge Posada and Bernie Williams do on April 23, 2000, that had never been done before in the majors?**
Both hit home runs from both sides of the plate in the same game—a first for teammates—in a 10–7 beating of the Blue Jays.

Q **Only one player got his 3,000th hit between 1925 and 1958. Who was he?**

Paul Waner, Boston Braves, June 19, 1942.

Q **Only once in big league history have two future Hall of Famers hit back-to-back home runs in the same inning** *twice in the same game.* **Who are they?**

Bill Terry and Mel Ott, New York Giants, August 13, 1932, in the first game of a doubleheader. They both homered in the fourth and again in the ninth inning, all off Sloppy Thurston of the Dodgers.

Q **What did Mo Vaughn, Tim Salmon, and Troy Glaus of the Anaheim Angels do on April 21, 2000, that had never been done before in big league history?**

In the fourth inning against Dwight Gooden at Tampa Bay, the trio homered. Then they all homered again in the ninth inning off Roberto Hernandez, as the Angels won 9–6. This was the first time in big league history that the same three men had homered (albeit not consecutively) in the same inning twice in the same game.

Q **"We hit at least 100 home runs in three different decades. Who are we?"**

Babe Ruth. From 1911 to 1920, he hit 103 homers; from 1921 to 1930, 462 (talk about being in his prime!); and from 1931 to 1940, he smacked another 140.

Frank Robinson. From 1951 to 1960, he hit 165 homers. From 1961–1970, he added another 310. From 1971 to 1976, he connected for 111 more home runs.

Hank Aaron. From 1951 to 1960, he hit 200 homers; from 1961 to 1970, 373; and from 1971 to 1976, 163 more home runs.

Q **Which member of the 3,000-hit club struck out the most?**
Lou Brock—3,023 hits, 1,730 strikeouts.

DON'T LEAVE EARLY DEPARTMENT

On April 29, 1932, Washington beat St. Louis 7–6 after both teams scored in the 9th, 10th, 11th, and 12th innings.

Q **Who has the most home runs as a Los Angeles Dodger?**
Eric Karros. He hit his 229th home run as a member of the Los Angeles Dodgers at home on June 13, 2000, breaking Ron Cey's record. Karros's blast was a solo shot off Matt Mantei of the Diamondbacks, leading LA to a 6–1 win.

Q **On April 15, 1942, Nick Etten, a wartime player with the Philadelphia Phillies, got his 14th hit in two weeks. How many were singles?**
None. All were extra-base hits.

Q **On June 3, 2000, Chris Turner of the New York Yankees homered in Atlanta. This was a rare example of a ballplayer homering in a park with which he shares a name—Turner homering in Turner Field. When else has this happened since 1900?**
Yes, there have been players named Briggs, but none of them homered in Briggs Stadium. Likewise, none of the Griffiths homered at Griffith Stadium; no Mack homered in Connie Mack Stadium. Steve Shea never homered at Shea Stadium. Neither did Shea Hillenbrand. Mike Busch never hit one out of Busch Stadium, and Terry Humphrey never launched one out of Humphrey Stadium. No Kauffman has homered at Kauffman Stadium, and no Jacobs has homered at Jacobs Field.

Until players with names like Comerica, Safeco, and Dodger come along, Dale Murphy retired the cup in this category, with 24 career home runs at Jack Murphy Stadium in San Diego. Dwayne Murphy hit one there, too, but Billy Murphy did not. And now that Jack Murphy Stadium is no more, Dale Murphy's record seems secure.

Q **On July 23, 2000, Lance Berkman of the Astros hit home runs in both the second and the seventh innings. What makes Berkman's feat unusual?**

The homers were off brothers: Andy and Alan Benes of the Cardinals. According to David Vincent, *the* authority on home runs, this was only the third time in major league history that one batter has homered off brothers in the same game.

The first time it happened was on September 24, 1922, when Rogers Hornsby of the Cardinals homered off both Jesse and Virgil Barnes of the New York Giants.

Hall of Famer Mike Schmidt of the Phillies homered off Paul and Rick Reuschel of the Cubs on April 17, 1976.

Q **Who hit the game-winning home run in the latest inning?**

Harold Baines of the Chicago White Sox, who homered in the 25th inning in a victory over the Milwaukee Brewers on May 8, 1984.

Q **Who had the highest single-season batting average while striking out at least 150 times?**

Sammy Sosa, 2001 Chicago Cubs. He hit .328 while striking out only 153 times. This broke Mo Vaughn's mark with the 1996 Red Sox when he hit .326 with only 154 whiffs.

Q **In which stadium were the most home runs hit?**

Detroit's old Tiger Stadium, which closed at the end of the 1999 season after 87 years: 11,113 home runs. Wrigley Field is a distant second.

Q **Only two men have hit both a home run and a triple in their first two big league plate appearances. Who are they?**

Frank Ernaga was the first man to accomplish this unusual feat. He broke in with the Cubs on May 24, 1957, but lasted just 29 games in two seasons.

The second man to homer and triple in his first two plate appearances was Alex Cabrera. He homered in his first big league at bat, June 26, 2000, for the Arizona Diamondbacks. He tripled the next day in his second at bat.

Q **The first four men who hit 45 homers, drove in 100 runs, and scored 150 runs in a season are Hall of Famers: Babe Ruth, Lou Gehrig, Joe DiMaggio, and Jimmie Foxx. Who is the fifth?**

Jeff Bagwell, 2000 Houston Astros: 47 home runs, 132 RBIs, and 152 runs scored.

Q **How many men have hit 40 home runs in a season in each league?**

Just five: Ken Griffey Jr., Mark McGwire, Darrell Evans, Shawn Green, and David Justice.

WAIT, I THINK I'M GETTING THE HANG OF THIS DEPARTMENT

Q **Morrie Rath of the Cincinnati Reds hit a home run in the seventh inning against the New York Giants on September 20, 1920. Although he had over 500 at-bats that year, his inside-the-parker was his first home run of the season. When did Rath hit his second homer of 1920?**

In the next inning—another inside-the-park home run.

Q **Who had the most hits before the All-Star game?**

Ralph Garr of the Atlanta Braves. Before the July 23, 1974, All-Star Game, he had 149 hits in 411 at-bats for a batting average of .363. His total for the season was 214 hits, tops in the league, with a batting average of .353.
Thanks to Lyle Spatz and Bill Deane for this one.

Q **Even though he could not buy a hit on September 20, 2000, Ben Petrick of the Rockies had a memorable day at the plate. What did he do?**

He drove in four runs with a sacrifice fly, a bases-loaded walk, and two groundouts.

Q **The only non–Hall of Famer to hit at least .360 for three consecutive years was Joe Jackson—until this man came along. Who is he?**

Larry Walker, Colorado Rockies: 1997, .366; 1998, .363; 1999, .379.

Q **Who hit the most home runs in a single season while having no more than 200 at-bats?**

It's a four-way tie at 16.

Batter	Team	HR	AB
Eddie Robinson	1955 Yankees	16	173
Bob Thurman	1957 Reds	16	190
Mike Simms	1998 Rangers	16	186
Russ Branyan	2000 Indians	16	193

Thanks to David Vincent, the expert on home runs.

Q **Which Canadian has the most hits?**

Larry Walker. On April 19, 2000, his single in an 8–7 loss by his Rockies to the Diamondbacks was his 1,447th hit, beating Jeff Heath's previous record. Walker is from Maple Ridge, British Columbia. Heath is a native of Fort William, Ontario.

Q **Which Hall of Famer hit the most home runs in a single season with fewer than 200 at-bats?**

Mickey Mantle, 1963 New York Yankees: 172 at-bats, 15 home runs.

In 1997, Mark McGwire hit 24 homers in 174 at-bats for the St. Louis Cardinals after his trade from the Oakland A's.

Q **The first three players to drive in at least 137 runs and walk at least 137 times in a season were all Hall of Famers: Babe Ruth (who did it five times), Ted Williams (twice), and Harmon Killebrew. Who was the fourth?**

Jason Giambi, 2000 Oakland Athletics: 137 RBIs, 137 walks.

Q **Only two players have started a season with back-to-back two–home run games. One is a Hall of Famer. The other one will be. Who are they?**

Eddie Mathews, 1958 Milwaukee Braves, and Barry Bonds, 2002 San Francisco Giants.

Q On August 21, 1931, Babe Ruth hit his 600th home run—the first man to reach that lofty plateau. On that date, which other players had hit 300, 400, or 500 home runs?

None. Rogers Hornsby was closest, with 293 homers on that date, just 307 back of the Babe.

Q When Cardinal Mark Whiten hit four home runs in a game on September 7, 1993, he finished the night with 12 runs batted in. How many runs did Mike Cameron drive in when he hit four home runs for the Mariners in Chicago on May 1, 2002?

Just four. Each of his homers came with the bases empty.

Q Cameron's four homers ties the record for most home runs in a game. But he created a brand new record, assisted by Bret Boone. Which record?

Cameron and Boone became the only teammates in history to hit two home runs each in the same inning. Each homered twice in the 10-run first inning, as the Mariners cruised to a 15–4 victory.

Q Who is the only man to hit 400 home runs for one team and at least 100 for another?

Barry Bonds. During his years with the Pittsburgh Pirates (1986–1992), Bonds hit 176 homers. He then went on to hit over 400 with the San Francisco Giants. Number 400 came on May 4, 2002, when he hit one in the first inning off Jimmy Haynes of the Cincinnati Reds.

Q **Only three men have hit 400 home runs for just one manager. Name the sluggers and their managers.**
Babe Ruth hit 516 homers for Miller Huggins, the Yankees manager, 1920–1929.
Think that *record will ever be broken?*
Mark McGwire hit 497 home runs for Tony LaRussa: 277 in Oakland and another 220 in St. Louis.
Barry Bonds. He hit over 400 for Dusty Baker of the San Francisco Giants.

GUYS WE'D LIKE TO INTRODUCE DEPARTMENT

Jason Giambi, meet Dave Stapleton. Giambi's batting average went *up* every year for his first seven years in the major leagues (with at least 500 at-bats per year). During his first seven years with the Boston Red Sox, Stapleton's batting average *declined* every year for six years.

Q **How many games did it take Manny Ramirez of the 2002 Boston Red Sox to hit a home run in each inning, 1 through 9?**
24.

Q **Since 1900, only four men have driven in over 1,100 runs in their careers without even one 100-RBI season. Who are they?**
Eddie Collins, Pete Rose, Mark Grace, and Rickey Henderson.

Q **Only one man has over 3,000 hits and played in more games than he had hits. Who is he?**
Rickey Henderson. Through 2004, he had 3,055 hits in 3,081 games.

Q **The first three men to hit a total of at least 100 home runs in their first three complete seasons in the major leagues are Hall of Famers: Joe DiMaggio (1936–1938, 107 homers); Ralph Kiner (1946–1948, 114 homers), and Eddie Mathews (1952–1954, 112 homers). Who is the fourth?**
Albert Pujols, St. Louis Cardinals, 2001–2003, 114.

Q **Who hit the most home runs in a single season without hitting a grand slam?**
Sammy Sosa. In 2001, none of his 63 homers was a grand slam.

Q **Who is the first major leaguer to hit at least 38 home runs in eight consecutive seasons?**
Rafael Palmiero: 1995, 39; 1996, 39; 1997, 38; 1998, 43; 1999, 47; 2000, 39; 2001, 47; 2002, 43. In 2003, he extended his record to nine with 38 home runs.

Q **Lots of big leaguers have hit at least 40 home runs in a single season. Who are the first two whose last names begin with the letter *O* who have accomplished that feat?**
Mel Ott: 42 homers, 1929 New York Giants.
Ben Oglivie: 41 homers, 1980 Milwaukee Brewers.

Q In 1937, Joe DiMaggio had 215 hits for the Yankees. Teammate Lou Gehrig hit 200. Who were the next two Yankees to have 200 hits each in the same season?

Bernie Williams (204) and Alfonso Soriano (209) in 2002.

THIS IS A TWO-PART QUESTION

Q 1. John Olerud of the New York Mets hit for the cycle (single, double, triple, home run) on September 11, 1997. How many other triples did he hit that year?

None.

Q 2. John Olerud, then with the Seattle Mariners, hit for the cycle again on June 16, 2001. How many other triples did he hit that year?

None.

JUNIORS AND SENIORS

Q **How old is the game of baseball as we know it today?**

Depends on whom you ask. According to the cover of the 2001 *International League Record Book*, professional baseball is ENTERING A THIRD MILLENNIUM.

That's old!

Q **Who is the oldest man ever traded?**

Jimmy Dykes. In August 1960, Dykes, the Detroit Tigers manager, was traded to the Cleveland Indians for their manager Joe Gordon. Gordon was 45. Dykes was 63.

Q **Who is the oldest nonpitcher to win a Gold Glove for the first time?**

Wade Boggs. He won it in 1994 as the third baseman for the New York Yankees. Boggs was 36 and had already played 12 years in the majors.

Q **Who is the youngest pitcher ever to record 30 saves in one season?**

Gregg Olson, Baltimore Orioles, 1990: 37 saves. Olson was 23.

Q **Who is the oldest pitcher to steal a base?**

Jim Kaat. He was 41 years and 8 months old when he did it in on June 23, 1980, with the St. Louis Cardinals. Steve Nicosia was catching for the Pirates in Pittsburgh, with Vicente Romo on the mound. As Kaat told us exclusively, "I had a lead in the bottom of the seventh and saw a chance to add to it. We won six to one. I went the distance!"
Thanks to Jim Kaat for this one—right from the source!

Q **Who is the oldest man to hit at least 20 home runs and steal 20 bases in a single season?**

Paul O'Neill. He was 38 with the 2001 New York Yankees when he hit 21 home runs and stole 22 bases.

TRICK QUESTION DEPARTMENT

Q **Who is the youngest player in history?**

Why, Omar Infante, of course. The youngest pitcher is probably Cy Young. Other contenders: Kid Gleason, Dmitri Young, Baby Ortiz, Babe Ruth, Harry Child, Kiddo Davis, and Ross Youngs. Do not add to this list: Dave Elder.

Q **At the age of 26 years, 269 days, Jimmie Foxx is the youngest man to hit 250 home runs. (He hit a total of 534 in his Hall of Fame career.) Who is the second youngest?**

Alex Rodriguez. A-Rod, playing for the Texas Rangers, hit #250 on April 30, 2002. He was 26 years, 277 days.

Q **Who are the oldest pitcher and batter to face each other who share the same last name and first initial?**

On April 8, 2004, John Franco (43) of the New York Mets faced Julio Franco (about 45) of the Braves. Their combined ages are 88.

It's All Relative

One of 9 kids—Greg Gagne, Curt Motton.

One of 10 kids—Willie McCovey, Drungo Hazewood, Esteban Yan, Dallas Williams.

One of 11 kids—Sammy Sosa (8 brothers and 2 sisters). Mariano Duncan has 7 brothers and 3 sisters. German Gonzales has 6 brothers and 4 sisters. Manny Alexander has 10 brothers.

One of 12 kids—Fred Breining.

One of 13 kids—Jim Essian, Bill Parker.

One of 14 kids—Dennis "Oil Can" Boyd (7 brothers, 6 sisters; his mother's name is Sweetie). Tony Armas Jr. (10 brothers and 3 sisters).

One of 15 kids—Jeff Stone, Bill Swift.

One of 16 kids—Jose Bautista, Jesus Sanchez. Ron Jackson told us that he is the fifth of 16 children.

Youngest of 21 kids—Willie Horton. (He wrote to tell us that he has 7 children of his own and 19 grandchildren.)

Ravelo Manzanillo has 31 brothers and 6 sisters.

Stop! We have a winner!

Q **Name a manager—a former big leaguer—whose son is a Demon.**
Jeff Torborg. His son Dale is a professional wrestler, known as "The Demon."

Pat Borders' five children all have names starting with the letter L.

Q **"I'm a major leaguer. My brother is an Elephant. Who are we?"**
Royce Clayton. His brother Royal, a career minor leaguer, played and coached for the Brother Elephants in Taiwan, 1996–1999.

Q **Only four father-and-son pitching pairs have played in the postseason. Name them.**
Jim Bagby Sr. (1920) and his son Jim Jr. (1946).
Paul "Dizzy" Trout (1940, 1945) and his son Steve (1984).
Mel Stottlemyre (1964) and his son Todd (1989, 1990, 1991, 1992, 1993, 1996, 1998, 1999).
Pedro Borbon Sr. (1982, 1973, 1975, 1976) and his son Pedro Jr. (1995).

Q **Which grandfather-grandson combination hit the most career home runs?**
Grandpa Bert Griffith and grandson Matt Williams. Griffith hit four homers during his brief career with the Dodgers and Senators, 1922–1924. Through 2004, Matt Williams hit 378 homers for the Giants, Indians, and Diamondbacks. Total: 382.

Q **Which Hall of Famers have hit home runs with their brothers *in the same game*?**
Hank Aaron and Tommie Aaron (who did it three times); Lloyd and Paul Waner (both Hall of Famers) (twice), Joe and Dom DiMaggio; Rick and Wes Ferrell (same inning).

Q **Name a major league general manager who was also the son-in-law of a general manager and the brother-in-law of a general manager.**

Roland A. Hemond. He married Margo Quinn, daughter of John Quinn, general manager of the Boston Braves before the team moved to Milwaukee, and remained in Milwaukee through 1958. Quinn was later general manager of the Philadelphia Phillies. John's son Bob was the general manager of the New York Yankees, the Cincinnati Reds, and the San Francisco Giants. Hemond himself served as the general manager of the Chicago White Sox and the Baltimore Orioles.

FATHER-IN-LAW	SON-IN-LAW
Judy Johnson	Billy Bruton
Lou Boudreau	Denny McLain
Juan Marichal	José Rijo
Herb Pennock	Eddie Collins Jr.
Harley Grossman	Harry Spilman
Ralph Branca	Bobby Valentine
August Busch	Eddie Mathews
Milton Stock	Eddie Stanky
Jerry Manuel	Rondell White
Denny Burns	Hank Wyse
George Gibson	Bill Warwick
Steve O'Neil	Skeeter Webb

BROTHERS-IN-LAW

Mike Easler, Cliff Johnson
Floyd Bannister, Greg Cochran
Rick Miller, married to Carlton Fisk's sister Janet
Doug Capilla, Bump Wills
Steve Blass, John Lamb
Ted Power, Joe Beckwith
Matt Herges, Todd Hollandsworth
Pol Perritt and his brother-in-law Jeff Tesreau were teammates on the New York Giants from 1915–1918.
Rick Reuschel, Scot Thompson
Roy Smalley Sr., Gene Mauch
Rube Bressler, Larry Kopf
Milt Gaston and Danny MacFayden, Red Sox teammates 1929–1931
Hall of Famers John Montgomery Ward and Tim Keefe were brothers-in-law and were teammates from 1885–1889 on the New York Giants. They entered the Hall together in 1964.
Coach Chuck Hernandez, Coach Nardi Contreras, Rich Monteleone

MARRIED TO SISTERS

Kirk Gibson and Dave Rozema married twin sisters Sandy and Joann Skalski, both strippers.
Tommy Hutton and Dick Ruthven, teammates on the Philadelphia Phillies, 1973–1975, married twin sisters Debbie and Sue Harper.

Dave Engel and Tom Brunansky married sisters.

Andre Thornton married Gail Jones, whose sister Phyllis married Pat Kelly; Thornton's wedding ceremony was performed by Rev. Howard O. Jones, her father.

I'M MY OWN GRANDPA DEPARTMENT

In 1940, Joe Haynes, a pitcher for the Washington Senators, was sold to the White Sox. He later married Thelma Griffith, the niece and the adopted daughter of Senators owner Clark Griffith. Thelma's brother was Calvin Griffith, Clark's nephew and adopted son. Calvin's brother was big leaguer Sherry Robertson. (Calvin's last name was changed when he was adopted by Clark.)

UNCLE–NEPHEW

Ray Hathaway, Dave Burba
Ernie Banks, Bob Johnson
Francis Healy, Fran Healy
Dwight Gooden, Gary Sheffield
Frank Shellenback, Jim Shellenback
Dan Driessen, Gerald Perry
Joe Henderson, Dave Henderson
Dick Schofield, Jayson Werth

STEPBROTHERS

Boog Powell and Carl Taylor
Joe Ausanio and Paul Runge

STEPFATHER–STEPSON

Jesus De La Rosa and Danny Bautista
Dennis Werth, Jayson Werth
Preston Wilson's stepfather is Mookie Wilson. Mookie married Preston's mother, who had been Mookie's sister-in-law. Thus, Mookie is both Preston's uncle and stepfather.

FATHERS OF TWINS

Pat Corrales, Mel Nieves, Alex Grammas, Jim Bunning, Buck Rogers, John Hudek, Mike Moore, Reds executive Jim Bowden, Hector Torres, Frank Baker (not the Hall of Famer), Mike Bordick, Sixto Lezcano, Bruce Tanner, Hall of Fame broadcaster Ernie Harwell

IS A TWIN

Jose and Ozzie Conseco, Russ Nixon, Tony Fernandez, Tom Brookens, Tom Murphy, Brian Doyle, Don Kirkwood

IS NOT A TWIN

Angels catchers Bengie Molina and his brother Jose are both listed as 27 years old in 2002, but they are not twins. They were born 10 months apart.

Q **Only once in major league history have brothers hit back-to-back home runs off the same pitcher. Who are they?**
Lloyd and Paul Waner, of the Pittsburgh Pirates, September 15, 1938. They both homered off Cliff "Mountain Music" Melton in a 7–2 victory over the New York Giants.

Q **How often does a father get to broadcast a game in which his son ties the father's career mark?**
On July 4, 2000, Tom Grieve, broadcasting for the Texas Rangers, watched as his son Ben, an outfielder with the Oakland A's, tied his mark with Ben's 65th career home run. Texas won 10–7.

Q **What was unusual about the fact that umpires Jerry Crawford, Mike DiMuro, and Brian Gorman worked the April 15, 2000, game between the Oakland A's and the Boston Red Sox?**
Each of these umpires is the son of a major league umpire—Shag Crawford, Lou DiMuro, and Tom Gorman.
   Thanks to Phyllis Otto of SABR's committee on umpires for this unusual tidbit.

Q **Name two baseball executives who were married to Oscar winners.**
Ted Turner, owner of the Atlanta Braves, was married to Jane Fonda. In 1971, she won an Oscar for her performance in the title role in *Klute*. She won again for *Coming Home* in 1978.
   Former Dodger Chairman and Chief Executive Officer Robert Daly's wife is Carole Bayer Sager, who won an Oscar in 1981 for writing "Arthur's Theme" ("Best That You Can Do") from the film *Arthur*.

Q **What's the connection: Mike Henneman, Bucky Dent, Jim Palmer, Glenn Davis, Mike Lum.**

They were all adopted. Davis grew up in the home of pitcher Storm Davis and took his family name.

Q **Just before the Mets-Rockies game on Mothers' Day, May 12, 2002, Chris Granozio, who operated the message board at Shea Stadium, visited both clubhouses. He wanted to ask the players their mothers' names so the board could say, for example, MO VAUGHN'S MOTHER'S NAME IS SHIRLEY as each player as came up to bat. What's the connection to The Archies?**

Granozio questioned Steve Trachsel and Mike Piazza, the Mets' starting battery. Their mothers' names, respectively, are Betty and Veronica.

Q **This player pinch hit for his brother *three times* one season. Who is he?**

On April 27, 2003, Bengie Molina pinch hit for his brother José vs. the Boston Red Sox at Anaheim. He popped out to second base in the seventh inning of a 14-inning game. On June 18 at Seattle, Bengie pinch hit for José and grounded into a 1-2-3 double play. Three days later, on June 21 at Los Angeles, Bengie pinch hit for José again and singled to right in the ninth.

Q **Who holds the major league record for most home runs in a single season by brothers (not necessarily teammates)?**

Jason and Jeremy Giambi. In 2002, Jason hit 41 for the Yankees, and Jeremy hit 20 for the Oakland A's and Phillies. Total: 61.

Q **Who are the only teammate brothers who homered in the same game three times *in one season*?**
Hank and Tommie Aaron, Milwaukee Braves. June 12, July 12 (in the same inning), and August 14, 1962.

Q **Who were the first teammate brothers to homer in the same inning *twice*?**
Billy and Cal Ripken Jr. The first time they did it, for the Orioles, was on September 15, 1990, in the fifth inning in a 4–3 loss to the Toronto Blue Jays.

They did it again on May 28, 1996, in the ninth inning in a 12–9 victory over Seattle.

Q **Which teammate brothers homered in the same game four times?** Hint: there are two correct answers—two pairs of brothers accomplished this unusual feat.

Vladimir and Wilton Guerrero, Monteal Expos. They did it on August 15, 1998, October 2, 1999, May 18, 2000, and again on September 18, 2000.

Jason and Jeremy Giambi also homered in the same game four times, all for the Oakland A's: May 8, 2000, September 15, 2000, June 21, 2001, and August 11, 2001.

Q **Which teammate brothers homered in the same game *three times* before any other pair of brothers ever did it even once?**
The Waners—Paul and Lloyd, both of the Pittsburgh Pirates.

On September 4, 1927, they became the first teammate brothers to homer in the same inning. They both connected again on June 9, 1929, and hit back-to-back homers on September 15, 1938.

MARRIED AT HOME PLATE

The first recorded home-plate wedding is said to have been that of the Cincinnati Reds groundskeeper Louis Rapp to Rosie Smith on the site of what would become Crosley Field in 1893.

Twenty-eight couples were married at home plate at Phoenix's Bank One Ballpark before the Brewers–Diamondbacks game on September 25, 2001. The event was a joint "Get Hitched at Home Plate" promotion by the Diamondbacks and the *Wedding Chronicle*, a Phoenix magazine devoted to nuptials. Over 100 people applied for the random drawing, and 28 couples were selected for the ballpark's first weddings. Each couple paid $495 and received 32 tickets for family and friends. Cake and photos were also included. The money ($13,860) went to Diamondbacks Charities. The ceremony was performed by Phillip Waring, a nondenominational Christian minister. A poll conducted by *The Wedding Chronicle* voted the Bank One Ballpark as Phoenix's #1 location to become engaged.

Chad Williams, a baseball fan from Bethlehem, Pennsylvania, proposed to Rachel Varkonyi in the gift shop of the Hall of Fame. With the help of gift-shop employees, Williams placed an engagement ring in a display case. While walking through the shop, she saw the ring and flowers, and Williams proposed. She accepted, and they were married in January 2002.

On June 7, 2002, 10 couples were married at Pringles Park, home of the West Tennessee Jaxx.

Seventy-two-year-old umpire Herm Arnoldink of Michigan's West Ottawa Baseball League and his wife were married at home plate at Holland High School on July 14, 1994.

Charlotte Pelon and Anthony Sanchez were married at Detroit's Tiger Stadium on October 14, 1984, right before the start of Game 5 of the World Series between the Tigers and the San Diego Padres. The Tigers won the game and the Series.

Matt Childers of the Mudville Nine and Francesca Mitchell were married at home plate at Billy Hebert Field in Stockton, California, on July 26, 2000, an off-day.

Mike Brown, assistant baseball coach at the University of Texas–Pan American and his wife, Claudette, were married at home plate at Golden Park in Columbus, Georgia (home of the RedStixx) before a South Atlantic League (Class A) All-Star Game on June 19, 1992.

The Lowell, Massachusetts, Spinners of the New York–Penn League helped a local radio station sponsor a married-at-home-plate promotion. Among the winners were Angela and Kevin Reid of Melrose, Massachusetts. The Reids got a free wedding on August 12, 1999, at Edward LeLacheur Park and a free honeymoon in Aruba. Lowell mayor Eileen Donoghue performed the ceremony. Among the on-field guests was the team mascot, the Canaligator.

On August 17, 2002, Heather Ying and Jeff Yang were married on the pitcher's mound of Richmond County Bank Ballpark, home of the Staten Island (New York) Yankees (New York–Penn League, Short-Season Class A). Hot dogs and sushi were served.

On June 1, 2002, Bobby Bartin and April Lewis were married in a candlelight ceremony at Whispering Pines soft-ball field in Inverness, Florida. The ceremony was performed by another softball player, who wore an umpire's uniform for the solemn occasion.

Bartin walked from the first-base dugout to the pitcher's mound and was then escorted by his groomsmen to home plate. The future Mrs. Bartin emerged from the third-base dugout and was walked to the mound. From there, she was escorted down a white carpet to home plate. Following the ceremony, the guests changed out of their formal wear and played a game of softball.

On July 20, 2002, Debbie Malette and Kevin Gerrard, both of Ottawa, Ontario, were married on the pitcher's mound at JetForm Park, home of the Lynx, the International League affiliate of the Montreal Expos. The wedding was part of a "Wedding in the Park" promotion, which included a mass renewal of vows for any married couples who wished to participate in the ceremonies on the field.

On November 12, 2002, Sheila Batton was called out to the pitcher's mound at Lee County Stadium (spring training home of the Twins) in Ft. Myers, Florida, to throw out the first pitch before a Carolina White Sox game against the St. Paul Saints in the Roy Hobbs League Veterans Division World Series.

After she did so, her boyfriend, Mike Harrison of the White Sox, walked out to the mound to join her. She thought he was going to propose, which he did on bended knee. Then out walked pastor Michael Grogan, wearing a Saints uniform (although he plays for the Fort Myers Hooters masters team). He performed the double-ring ceremony for the happy and surprised couple on the pitcher's mound surrounded by both teams. Harrison went one for two with a walk as the White Sox won 12–1.

On August 28, 1947, Joe Fonta, manager of the Smithfield-Selma Leafs in the Tobacco State League, was married in his Leafs uniform at Legion Field's home plate to Ruth Wiggs. Players created a canopy of crossed bats for the happy couple.

On April 25, 1970, David Lowe and Pamela Jo Schuster were married at home plate at Riley Field, Sumter, South Carolina, home of the Sumter Indians, a Cleveland farm club for which Lowe was a pitcher. Colonel John Ellis, an air force chaplain in his dress whites, performed the solemn ceremony. The couple walked under crossed bats held by the Indians and the Anderson (South Carolina) Senators.

COUPLE WHO SHOULD GET MARRIED AT HOME PLATE DEPARTMENT

Casey Daigle, of the Arizona Diamondbacks, and his fiancée Jenny Finch, All-American softball pitcher from the University of Arizona, 2004 Olympic Gold Medalist, and a host of *This Week in Baseball*.

Legendary baseball executive Roland A. Hemond told us that when he learned of the home-plate wedding of Jerry Hairston Sr. and Esperanza Arelcano during winter ball in Hermosillo, Sonora, Mexico, he remembered that Hairston was a switch-hitter. Hemond wondered which side of the plate Hairston stood on during the ceremony.

Hemond was present for Don Zimmer's home-plate wedding at Elmira, New York, on August 16, 1951. Hemond was working for the Hartford Chiefs. In the game that followed the wedding, Hemond reports that right hander Elmer Toth of the Chiefs knocked Zimmer down with a pitch in the bottom of the first. But Zimmer singled on the next pitch.

Thanks to Roland A. Hemond for these great memories.

The date: October 6, 2003.

The place: Ripken Stadium in Aberdeen, Maryland, home of the Ironbirds.

The couple: Dave Bard, who works for the team, and Melissa Tolson. The couple was married under a traditional Jewish *chuppah*, a canopy. This was one of the few Jewish home-plate ceremonies. A photo of the ceremony and a list of the members of the bridal party (including the flower girls and ring bearer) is available at http://ironbirdsbaseball.com/news/?id=3865.

Debbie and Tom Watterson renewed their vows (they've been married for 29 years) on the pitcher's mound at LaGrave Field in Ft. Worth, Texas, home of the Cats in the independent Central League. Stray Cat, the unordained team mascot, performed the ceremony.

OUCH!

Darren Oliver of the Texas Rangers was already on the disabled list because of an ailing left shoulder when he fell through the floor of his attic while rummaging around. He needed 12 stitches to close a cut on his right leg, an injury that added five days to his stay on the disabled list.

Q **Name a future Hall of Famer whose nose was broken by a teammate.**

Cal Ripken Jr. He was standing next to Roberto Hernandez, posing for the 1996 American League All-Star team photograph. When Hernandez slipped and lost his balance, he flailed his arms. His hand hit Ripken right in the nose and broke it—and Ripken still didn't break stride in his consecutive game streak.

Carlos Perez of the Expos was driving his car, trying to pass the team bus. He was in an accident and broke his nose.

Dwight Gooden missed a start with the Mets when teammate Vince Coleman hit him with a golf club in the clubhouse.

Rick Reed of the Twins missed a start against his old team, the Mets, on June 18, 2002, because he cut a finger on his pitching hand while opening the zipper on a traveling bag.

Greg Harris of the Texas Rangers injured his wrist flicking sunflower seeds.

Charlie Hough broke his pinky shaking hands "pinky-style."

After hearing a motivational speaker, Steve Sparks was inspired. Inspired to try tearing a phone book in half, he dislocated his shoulder.

Jason Isringhausen of the A's punched a trashcan and broke his hand.

John Smoltz tried ironing his own shirt—*while he was wearing it*. He burned his chest.

In June 2000, Philadelphia relief pitcher Jason Boyd was so frustrated after the Phillies' loss to the Marlins that he slammed his glove in the dugout, breaking a bone in his pitching hand. He was out for 15 days.

Yankee third-base coach Willie Randolph missed an August 2000 game with a broken rib, sustained when he was hit during batting practice.

David Justice missed two games in 2000 with a sore neck after sleeping awkwardly.

OUCH!

Oakland A's manager Art Howe was injured while running out of the dugout to argue a call with an umpire.

On May 15, 1999, Rangers pitcher Esteban Loaiza broke his right hand by slamming it in a car door. He returned to the team on July 5.

On July 1, 1994, Joe Oliver, then with the Reds, cut his right (throwing) arm while unloading his dishwasher at home. He needed seven stitches.

Henry Cotto of the New York Yankees was cleaning his ears with a cotton swab while sitting on the bench in the dugout. Ken Griffey Sr. bumped into him, and Cotto's eardrum was ruptured.

Jim Barr broke his hand in 1979 punching what he thought was a picture of a toilet seat on a sign held by a fan. It was not a picture.

Ryan Klesko of the San Diego Padres was injured on September 17, 2001, while helping the grounds crew unfurl a large American flag during pregame ceremonies at Qualcomm Stadium. He reinjured his back. Yes, that's the same Ryan Klesko who once pulled a muscle picking up a lunch tray. Padres manager Bruce Bochy also fell while walking backward.

Brian Anderson cut the middle finger on his pitching hand while opening a bottle of cologne.

Match these players with their unusual injuries (one player accounts for two of these injuries).

A. Bobby Grich

B. Rick Aguilera

C. Adam Eaton

D. Nolan Ryan

E. Steve Sparks (He was out for an entire season.)

F. Ricky Bones

G. Bobby Ojeda

H. Curt Simmons

I. Rickey Henderson

J. Danny Cox

K. Wade Boggs

L. Marty Cordova

M. Tom Glavine

N. Mark Smith

O. Paul Molitor

P. Kevin Mitchell

Q. Thomas Howard

R. Terry Harper

S. Adam Eaton

1. Recliner injury

2. Lost part of a finger using a hedge clipper

3. Lifting an air conditioner

4. Jumping from a wall to the beach while fishing

5. Lost part of a toe to a lawn mower

6. Lifting a suitcase

7. Ripping a phone book in half

8. Falling down the stairs at home while carrying his suitcase on the way to the airport

9. Stabbing himself while trying to open a DVD case

10. Hurt his eyelid because he "slept wrong"

11. Burned his face at a tanning salon

12. Coyote bite

13. Frostbite—in August

14. Inability to blink

15. Injured putting on boots

16. Sprained ankle stepping on a baseball while shagging flies

17. Stabbed himself in the stomach (two stitches) trying to open a DVD package

18. High-fiving

T. Chris Brown
U. John Stearns
V. José Cardinal

19. Couldn't sleep because chirping crickets kept him awake
20. Broke a rib vomiting bad airplane food
21. Pulled a muscle vomiting
22. Dislocated a knuckle while his hand was stuck in another player's glove
23. Stuck his hand into a broken air conditioner

1F, 2G, 3A, 4J, 5H, 6B, 7E, 8Q, 9C, 10T, 11L, 12D, 13I, 14V, 15K, 16U, 17S, 18R, 19V, 20M, 21P, 22O, 23N

Honorable mention: Luis Castillo, who once set off a hotel's fire alarm because he thought it was a shampoo dispenser.

On October 7, 2002, in the final game of the American League Division Series, Denny Hocking went 2–4 with an RBI and caught a pop-up for the final out of the Twins' 5–4 victory over the Oakland Athletics. While he was celebrating in a pile with the rest of the Twins, a teammate stepped on his right hand, cutting his middle finger and finishing his season. Hocking called the injury "bittersweet."

Kevin Brown was dissatisfied with his own performance on September 3, 2004. So he did what any other $15,000,000 per year pitcher would do. He punched a clubhouse wall with his left (non-pitching) hand and broke his third and fifth metacarpal bones. Pins were inserted during surgery. Brown missed 20 games.

DON'T YOU HATE WHEN THAT HAPPENS? DEPARTMENT

Julio Franco broke the middle finger of his left hand on August 19, 2003, in the Atlanta weight room while he was talking with a teammate. An 80-pound dumbbell rolled over the finger.

Satoru Komiyama injured his finger trying to open his garage door.

Mark Quinn tripped over a table in his home while playing kung fu with his brother. He cracked a rib.

Jason Johnson broke a finger on his pitching hand while practicing his pitching motion. He jammed his finger into the ground.

Pokey Reese's injured finger was being worked on by a trainer when the trainer accidentally pulled the finger and reinjured it.

Kevin Brown's son was falling off a bed. Brown reached to catch him and injured his back.

Juan Rivera ran into a golf cart while shagging fly balls during batting practice. He broke his right kneecap.

Kazuhiro Sasaki went on the disabled list after injuring his ribs carrying a suitcase up a flight of stairs in his home.

Freddy Garcia ruptured an eardrum by sneezing on a plane.

Terry Mulholland required eight stitches in his head for an injury sustained celebrating the Braves' victory over the Mets in the 1999 National League Championship Series. He jumped up so high that he hit his head on cement.

On March 5, 2004, during spring training, Yankee John Flaherty dislocated his left thumb while breaking in a new catcher's mitt. The new mitt did not have a thumb guard.

Lyle Overbay suffered a serious facial injury in January 2003 during a soft-toss drill.

In 1996 Jacques Jones suffered a season-ending knee injury in his first professional game. He was playing for the Fort Myers Miracle, the Twins affiliate in the Florida State League, Class A Advanced.

Jason Grimsley lost his left big toe in a motorcycle accident when he was 12.

On May 19, 2002, Matt Anderson shredded a muscle in his right armpit while throwing an octopus.

Stop! We have a winner.

WHAT'S IN A NAME?

PLAYERS WE'D LIKE TO INTRODUCE TO EACH OTHER DEPARTMENT

Ron Mahey, a graduate of Alan B. Shepard High School in Palos Heights, Illinois, meet Aaron Scheffer, a graduate of John Glenn High School in Westland, Michigan.

Jim Derrington, meet Trent Durrington.

Travis Driskill, meet Darryl Strawberry.

Jimmy Gobble, meet Turkey Stearnes.

Bump Wills, say hi to Nate Bumps.

Ivan Coffie, meet Pasqual Coco.

Mark Ballinger, meet Mark Belanger.

Scott Service and Scott Servais.

Joe Girardi, meet Joe Erardi.

Jim Leland and Jim Leland Barr.

Dennis Eckersley, meet Dennis Tankersley.

Jay Howell, this is Jay Powell.

"Dirty" Alan Gallagher, meet "Bruno" Betzel. Oh, sorry. Let's be more formal: Alan Mitchell Edward George Patrick Henry Gallagher, meet Christian Frederick Albert John Henry David Betzel.

Jim Kaat, say hello to Don Heffner. Kaat pitched 898 games in the majors from 1959 to 1983, during which time seven men occupied the White House: Dwight Eisenhower, John Kennedy, Lyndon Johnson, Richard Nixon, Gerald Ford, Jimmy Carter, and Ronald Reagan. Heffner played 743 games in the majors from 1934 to 1944 while just *one man* was president—Franklin D. Roosevelt.

Thanks to Lee Sinins for alerting us to Heffner's odd and unbreakable record.

Q **Who is the greatest artist in the history of baseball?**
Mike Colangelo.
What—you were going to guess Lance Painter?

Q **Who is the best journalist in baseball?**
Jimmy Journell.

Q **The most common nickname in baseball is "Lefty." Can you name a "Lefty" who threw righty?**
Phil "Lefty" Leftwich.

Q **Who is the most dangerous player in the majors?**
David Riske.

Q **What is the only team name that has been used by professional teams in baseball, football, hockey, and basketball?**

Pittsburgh Pirates.

Baseball: The Pittsburgh Pirates have been so named in the National League since 1889.

Football: The Pittsburgh Steelers of the National Football League started life in 1933 as the Pirates.

Hockey: The year 1924 saw the birth of the Pittsburgh Pirates of the National Hockey League. During the 1930–1931 season, the team moved to Philadelphia and became the Quakers, but they lasted there just one season.

Basketball: The Pittsburgh Pirates played in the National Basketball League for just one season, 1938–1939.

Q **Vida Blue made his major league debut with the Oakland A's on July 20, 1969. Why was this story buried in the back of the Oakland newspapers—in fact, in the back of *every* paper?**

Because on that day, July 20, 1969, Neil Armstrong made *his* debut as a moon walker.

TYPESETTERS' NIGHTMARE DEPARTMENT

Jeriome Robertson, Jhonny Peralta, Andruw Jones, Jeromy Burnitz.

Q **What is Jeff Manto's nickname?**

Mickey.

Q **How many major leaguers can you name whose first names rhyme with their last names?**

Ed Head, Mark Clark, Lu Blue, Heine Meine, Bill McGill, Still Bill Hill, Turk Burke, Cy Pieh, Hill Billy Bildilli, Greg Legg, and Don Hahn.

THE ALL-DENTAL TEAM

Lip Pike, Brian Mochler, Bucky Dent (twice), Charlie Root, Lew Drill, Yank Terry, John Smiley, Rocky Bridges, Sam Dente, Bob Brush, Sam "Toothpick" Jones, Choo Freeman.

Manager: Leo "The Lip" Durocher.

EVEN THEN HE KNEW DEPARTMENT

Ted Spencer, chief curator at the Baseball Hall of Fame, was named for Ted Williams.

Q **Only two players in Yankee history have had last names which start with the letter I. They were teammates. Who were they?**

Hideki Irabu and Pete Incaviglia. Both were with the Yankees in 1997.

Q **Name the only major league team whose city name and team name are both in a foreign language.**

San Diego Padres.

Q **Which major leaguer went to the least expensive high school?**

Calvin Maduro, a graduate of Tourist Economy School in Santa Cruz, Aruba.

Billy Ripken has a dog named "Dog."

MINOR-LEAGUERS WE HOPE MAKE IT TO THE MAJORS DEPARTMENT

Cesar King (who can be on the "leader" team twice), Boof Bonzer, Guiseppe Chiarmonte, Gil Scharringhausen, Dean Brueggemann, Nehames Bernstine, John-Ford Griffin, Jay Sborz, Kody Kirkland, Felix Pie, Chadd Blasko, Colt Griffin, Matt Allegra, Maxim St. Pierre, Tomas Joseph Lyons, Rocky Cherry, Arturo Bravo, Gbenga Olayemi, Mike Paradis, Jon-Michael Gold, John VanBenschoten, Aarom Baldiris—whose first name is derived by spelling half his mother's first name (Moraima) backward and adding an "a." (Here's $10 that says his first name will be rendered "Aaron" at least 10 times during his rookie season!)—Chuck Tiffany, and Joe Soprano.

The all-terrain team now includes Hilly Hathaway and Trench Davis.

Q **Athletes who have appeared on Wheaties boxes have included Olympic champions and American World Cup winners. This guy, a .252 hitter during his major league career, appeared on a Wheaties box in 2002. Who is he?**
Jim Thorpe.

Q **A number of ballplayers were known by their middle names rather than their true first names. Examples are Henry Louis Gehrig and Dudley Mike Hargrove. Match the players on the left, who went by their middle names, with their true first names on the right.**

1. Clise Dudley   A. Bertram
2. Tim McCarver   B. Charlton
3. Roger Clemens   C. Jacinto

4.	Ray Fontenot	D.	George
5.	Damion Easley	E.	Franz
6.	Paul Bako	F.	Elzie
7.	Dante Bichette	G.	Walter
8.	Lum Davenport	H.	William
9.	Scarborough Green	I.	Silton
10.	Atlee Hammaker	J.	Robert
11.	Julian Javier	K.	Steven
12.	Otto Knabe	L.	Anthony
13.	Clyde Milan	M.	Colonel
14.	Buster Mills	N.	Manuel
15.	Jouette Meekin	O.	Virle
16.	Nomar Garciaparra	P.	Clifford
17.	Kevin McReynolds	Q.	Jesse
18.	Rance Mulliniks	R.	Maryland
19.	Gene Rounsaville	S.	Thomas
20.	Roe Skidmore	T.	Alphonse
21.	Nolen Richardson	U.	James
22.	Finners Quilan	V.	Joubert
23.	Dykes Potter	W.	Gabor

1F, 2U, 3H, 4I, 5C, 6V, 7T, 8W, 9A, 10B, 11N, 12E, 13Q, 14M, 15D, 16L, 17G, 18K, 19O, 20J, 21P, 22S, 23R

Q **Name a big leaguer who appeared in the films *The Graduate* and *Camelot*.**
Tom House. He also appeared in television's *Rat Patrol* and *Hogan's Heroes* as an extra.

Pitcher Steve Schrenk has five children. Like Roger Clemens's children, all of Schrenk's children have names that start with the same letter: Kali Katrice, Kodi, Konor, Kenzi, and Kollin. Meet Boog Powell's family: John, his wife Janet, and their children John Jr., Jennifer, and Jill.

Perhaps the Powells would like to meet Darrell Johnson's family: Darrell, his wife Dixie, and their children Dara, Denise, Deana, and Douglas. Hey, what about the Giambis? Parents John and Jeanne and their children Jason, Jeremy, and Julie.

If Gorrell Robert Stinson ever got into trouble, it would make it hard for *every* kid named Gorrell.

GUYS WHOSE NICKNAME SHOULD BE "HAPPY" DEPARTMENT

Cardell Camper.
The manager of the Winston-Salem Warthogs, the Chicago White Sox affiliate in the Class A Advanced Carolina
    League, is Ken Dominguez. His wife's name is NanC.
Willie Crawford has a daughter named Holidae.
Manny Trillo has a daughter named Aloha.
Otis Nixon's daughter is named Genesis.
Fred McGriff's children are named Erick and Ericka.
Milt May's daughter is Merrily.
Russ Nixon's daughters include Misty and Rebel.

Lou Whittaker has a daughter named Asia.
Dave Burba's wife's name is Star.
Cecil Fielder's son is Prince.
Ivan Rodriguez has a daughter named Ivanna.
Marty Pevey has a son named Ringo.
Luis Polonia's son is named Rotney.
Mike Veeck's son is named Nitro.
John Russell has a son named Steel.
Jim Traber has a child named Trabes.
Felix Jose has two sons named Felix: Felix Jr. and Felix III.
Benito Santiago has two sons named Benito and a daughter named Bennybeth.
Dr. Joseph Bosco, associate team physician for the New York Mets, has a son named Bear.
Dave Hudgens has a son named Rock.
Umpire Joe Brinkman has a daughter named Honey Joe.
Minor league coach Gregg Ritchie has a daughter named Arizona.

Q **Name a major leaguer who toured with the Professional Bowlers Association.**
Bill Sudakis.

Q **How did Lindy McDaniel get his first name?**
He was named for Charles A. Lindbergh, nicknamed "Lucky Lindy." McDaniel was born in 1935, eight years after Lindberg's historic solo flight from New York to Paris. Lindbergh, an extremely skilled pilot, hated the name "Lucky."

Q **What's the connection: James White, Grover Cleveland Jones, John Donahue, Cornell Jones, Edward Van Buren, Charles Phillippe, James McGuire.**
They all shared the same nickname—"Deacon."

Q **Who is the best player in history?**
Karl Best. Perhaps he's a friend of Champ Summers, Bill Champion, Victory Faust, and Win Kelum. Probably not a friend of Losing Pitcher Mulcahy.

Q **Who is the most devout ballplayer?**
Reggie Baldwin, whose true first name is "Reverend." Perhaps he was a friend of Deacon Jones or Pius Schwert. Probably not a friend of José Pagan.

IF THEY MARRIED DEPARTMENT

If Bing Miller married Jung Bong, he'd be Bing Bong.
If Happy Chandler married Newt Halliday, he'd be Happy Halliday.

HOW DID HE GET THAT NICKNAME? DEPARTMENT

Q **How did Robert Belinsky get the nickname "Bo"?**
A fighter as a youth, the nickname derives from boxer Carl "Bobo" Olson.

YOU CAN'T MAKE THIS STUFF UP DEPARTMENT

Prominent Santa Monica California attorney Michael Monk was a part owner of the Padres.

Q **Who is the most standup, substantial, upright, honest, solid player in the majors?**
Kevin Mench.

Q **On June 12, 1989, Tim Jones of the Cardinals did something that nobody in the majors had done in over 100 years. What did he do?**
In a game against the Chicago Cubs, Jones caught—the first catcher in the majors named Jones since Bill Jones caught for the Philadelphia Keystones in 1884 in the Union Association.

Q **Who was the first designated hitter who really was a "DH"?**
Danny Heep.

One of the longest names in baseball belongs to Yankee Dane Sardinha. While his last name is only eight letters long, his middle name is Kiheimahanaomauiakeo—20 letters—Hawaiian for "long cloak of Maui."

Q **Name two big leaguers with apostrophes in their first names.**
D'Arcy Raymond "Jake" Flowers and D'Angelo Jiminez.

STATE DEPARTMENT

Minor league prospect John Maine, Arky Vaughn, Herb Washington, Washington Fullmer, Jersey Bakely, Tex Jones, Cal Ripken Jr., Del Crandall.

Honorable mentions: Lon Warneke, the "Arkansas Hummingbird"; Ty Cobb, the "Georgia Peach"; Ron Guidry, "Louisiana Lightning"; minor leaguer Mike "Missisippi" Smith, to differentiate him from Mike "Tex" Smith, both in the Reds organization; Turk Wendell's daughter Dakota.

When Adam Riggs made his second appearance for the Anaheim Angels on August 16, 2003, his uniform misspelled the name of his team. His shirt said ANGEES instead of ANGELS.

Q **Only once in big league history has a team featured two players named Butch at the same time. Which team and which players?**

The 1982 New York Yankees. The players were Clell "Butch" Hobson and Harold "Butch" Wynegar.

Butch Metzger and Butch Benton were both on the 1979 New York Mets, but not simultaneously.

Q **Can you name a guy who wore his *first* name on his cap on the field?**

Umpire Al Clark. His cap said "AL," for American League.

YOU CAN'T MAKE THIS STUFF UP DEPARTMENT

On April 29, 2003, Mike Redmond of the Florida Marlins pinch-hit for Mark Redman.

Redman, #55, is a pitcher. His nickname is "Red."

Redmond, #52 is a catcher. His nickname is "Red."

Q **Which minor league prospect is most likely to succeed?**

Cameron Likely.

Q **How many teams can you name which featured three "Reds" at the same time?**

It's a five-way tie:

The New York Giants of 1909 was the first team with three players nicknamed Red at the same time. They were Red Murray, Red Ames, and Red Waller.

The 1910 St. Louis Browns featured Red Corriden, Red Fisher, and Red Nelson.

The 1915 Cincinnati Reds team included Red Killefer, Red Ames, and Red Dooin.

Red Roberts, Red Marion, and Red Barbary were teammates on the 1943 Washington Senators.

The 1946 St. Louis Cardinals included Red Schoendienst, Red Barrett, and Red Munger.

The 1909 Giants were one of the great nickname teams of all time: Admiral Schlei, Moose McCormick, Buck Herzog, Tillie Shafer, Hooks Wiltse, Bugs Raymond, Rube Marquard, Doc Crandall, Bull Durham, and Laughing Larry Doyle. The team finished the season 92–61, in third place.

THREE POLITICALLY INCORRECT NICKNAMES ON THE SAME TEAM DEPARTMENT

Q **Which team had three players nicknamed "Dummy"?**

The New York Giants of 1901: George Michael "Dummy" Leitner, William John "Dummy" Deegan, and Luther Haden "Dummy" Taylor.

Q **Carlos Lee is an outfielder with the Chicago White Sox. His younger brother is a minor leaguer in the White Sox system. What's his name?**
Carlos Lee.

WHAT'S THE NAME OF YOUR TEAM? DEPARTMENT

Angel Moreno played for the Angels.

Dave Philley played for the Phillies.

José Cardenal was a Cardinal. So was Conrad Cardinal. Red Bird was not.

Garland Buckeye played for the Cleveland Indians (Ohio is the Buckeye state). "Indian" Bob Johnson did not. Neither did Birdie Cree.

Red Ames and Red Lucas were Reds.

Doc White and Ed White were White Sox.

The St. Louis Browns had six Browns: Willard Brown, the other Willard Brown, Curly Brown, Elmer Brown, Lloyd Brown, and Walter Brown. Ed Brown played for the Brown Stockings.

Red Rollings, Red Ruffing, and Red Shannon were all Red Sox.

The Blue Jays have not had a player named Jay.

While the Tampa Bay Devil Rays have not had a player named Ray, they have had Rey Ordoñez.

The Brewers have never had a Brewer.

Neither Yank Robinson nor Yank Terry played for the Yankees.

Daryl Boston did not play in Boston. Likewise, Reggie Cleveland did not play in Cleveland.

Tyler Houston never played for the Houston Astros.

Big Ed Delahanty was not a Giant. Neither was Wee Willie Keeler. Big Edd Roush was.

Neither Johnny Priest nor Eddie Priest, nor even Dave Pope ever played for the Cardinals or the Padres. Nor did Len, Bubba, or Hi Church. And of course, neither José nor Dave Pagan was ever a Padre, a Cardinal, or an Angel. But Johnny Podres was a Padre.

Spider Clark, Spider Jorgenson, and Spider Wilhelm never played for the Cleveland Spiders.

Rocky Colavito, Rocky Coppinger, and Rocky Nelson—never Rockies.

Marlin Stuart never played for the Marlins.

Tiny Chaplin was a Giant, but not a Padre or a Cardinal.

Buck Showalter did not manage the Pittsburgh Pirates—the "Bucs."

Doug Bird was neither a Cardinal, a Blue Jay, nor an Oriole.

Gary Beare did not play for the Cubs.

Joe Astroth—not an Astro. Dick Star was not an Astro, either.

Twink Twining was not a Twin.

Senator Jim Bunning (R-Ky.) did not play for the Senators, but Marvin E. Throneberry was a Met.

WHO ARE THESE GUYS? DEPARTMENT

One of the best-known double-play combinations in baseball is Tinker, Evers, and Chance. As far as names go, one of the best outfield combinations is Alou, Alou, and Alou.

See if you know these guys à la the *Jeopardy* format—that is, state your answer in the form of a question.

Q **Warren Ogden, Mr. Berg, and Lyn Lary.**
Who are Curly, Moe, and Lary?

Q **George Bell, John Powell, Casey.**
Who are Bell, Boog, and Candaele?

Q **Pee Wee, Joe Crede, and Hazen Shirley.**
Who are Reece, Crede, and Cuyler?

Q **Albert Schoendienst, Bill White, and Vida.**
Who are Red, White, and Blue?

Q **Tommy John, Gabe Paul, Lefty George, and Frank Ringo.**
Who are the Beatles of baseball?

Q **Ken Crosby, Lena Styles, Cotton Nash, Irv Young.**
Who are Crosby, Styles, Nash, and Young?

Q **Sam Faith, Sam Hope, and George Sharrott if he muffs a play.**
Who are Faith, Hope, and Sharrott-E?

Q **Dick Tomanek, Turk Farrell, and Jay Pettibone.**
Who are Tom, Dick, and Harry?

Q **Harry Lowery, Tom Butters, Smead Jolley.**
Who are Peanuts, Butters, and Jolley?

Q **George Henry Schlei, James Joseph Stafford, Ralph Houk, Joe, Mr. Cottrell, Jason Szuminski, Jim Field, Joe Marshall, Gary Mathews, Gary Mathews Jr.**
Name the all-military team: Admiral, General, the Major, Sargent, Ensign, Captain, Field Marshall, Sarge, Little Sarge.

Broadcaster: Bob Elson, the Commander.

Owner: Colonel Jacob Ruppert.

13

WHAT'S THE CONNECTION?

Q **Jeff Bagwell, José Canseco, John Kruk, Jeff Torborg, Lou Piniella, Matt Williams, Billy Gardner, Bo Belinsky, Don Blasingame, Joe Pepitone, Ted Williams, Benji Gil, David Justice, Tony Alvarez, Aaron Boone.**

Each of these players is or was married to a beauty queen.

Jeff Bagwell's former wife Shaune was a beauty queen. She is probably one of the few baseball wives with her own website: www.shaunebagwell.com.

José Canseco's ex-wife Esther Haddad was Miss Miami when they married in October 1988.

John Kruk and Jeff Torborg are each married to former Miss New Jerseys: Mrs. Kruk, (Melissa McLaughlin, Miss New Jersey USA 1999) and Mrs. Torborg (Suzie Barber, Miss New Jersey 1960).

Lou Piniella, a native of Tampa, married Anita Garcia, Miss Tampa 1962.

Matt Williams's ex-wife Michelle Johnson was 1982's International Model of the Year.

Billy Gardner's wife, the former Barbara Camaroli, was a Miss Connecticut.

Bo Belinsky's first wife was Jo Collins, Playboy's Miss December 1964. She was Playboy's Playmate of the Year for 1965.

Don Blasingame's wife, Sara, daughter of Walker Cooper, was Miss Missouri 1957.

Joe Pepitone's wife, Steevie Deeker, was a Playboy Bunny.

Ted Williams's first wife, Delores Wettach, was a Miss Vermont.

Before becoming Miss Texas 1995, Benji Gil's wife, Carly Jarmon, was Miss Teen Texas and also Miss Teen Hurst-Euless-Bedford. She was the first Miss Teen Texas to become Miss Texas.

David Justice was married to Oscar-winner Halle Berry. She won the Miss Teen All-American Pageant in 1985. She was also first runner-up in the Miss USA Pageant and won the evening-gown competition at the 1986 Miss World contest.

Tony Alvarez, of the Pittsburgh Pirates, is married to Astrid Carolina Herrera of Venezuela, Miss World 1984.

Aaron Boone's wife, Laura Cover, was Playboy's Miss October 1998.

Former minor leaguer Casey Close, later an agent for many players, married Gretchen Carlson, Miss America 1989.

Q Vincent Van Gogh, Grover Cleveland Alexander.

Van Gogh cut off his own ear. Alexander had cancer in his right ear, and it was amputated.

Q Darren Dreifort, Jose Rijo, Chad Fox, Nate Bland, Lance Carter.

These pitchers each had "Tommy John" surgery twice.

Q Ray Knight and Orlando Peña.

Both married women named Nancy Lopez.

Q Johnny Oates and Leo Cardenas.

Both married women named Gloria Jackson.

Q Dennis Martinez, Mike Morgan, Jesse Orosco, Rick Reuschel, and Frank Tanana.

They surrendered home runs to both Bobby and Barry Bonds.

Q Mark Koenig, Yats Wuestling, Lyn Lary, Red Rolfe, George Stirnweiss, Frank Crosetti, Jerry Kenney, Bobby Murcer, Wayne Tolleson, Mike Gallego, Tim Foli, and Derek Jeter.

They all wore #2 for the New York Yankees.

Q Eddie Grant, Christy Mathewson, Lou Gehrig, Billy Sunday, John McGraw, and Abner Doubleday.

Each had a World War II Liberty Ship, part of the U.S. Merchant Marines, named for him. The "Lou Gehrig," ship number MCE 210, was built in Portland, Maine, and was launched on January 17, 1943. It transported cargo and soldiers for the D-Day invasion of Normandy, June 6, 1944. The "Lou Gehrig" was scrapped off Kearny, New Jersey, in 1966.

Q **Dieon Sanders, Derek Jeter, Bob Uecker, and George Steinbrenner.**

They all hosted *Saturday Night Live*.

Q **Mickey Mantle, Shigetoshi Hasegawa, Salome Barojas, José Valdivielso, and Alvaro Espinoza.**

During his 50-plus years as the public address announcer at Yankee Stadium (starting with Mickey Mantle's very first game on April 17, 1951), Bob Sheppard has pronounced thousands of names, including the names of over 700 Yankees. These names were, in order, his favorite to pronounce.

Q **Terry Puhl, Ed Sprague Sr., Kevin Hickey, Manny Sanguillen, Dave McNally, Ed Ott, Ruppert Jones, Bob Bailor, Bill Melton, Scot Thompson, Moises Alou, Jerry Spradlin, Zane Smith, Ron Guidry, Erik Bedard, and Pat Meares.**

None of these big leaguers played baseball in high school—mostly, because their schools did not have baseball teams.

Terry Puhl: The Comprehensive School in Melville, Saskatchewan, was not comprehensive enough to have a baseball team.

Ed Sprague Sr. did not play *any* sport in high school.

Kevin Hickey played 16-inch softball (a Chicago tradition) and led his team, the Bobcats, to the national championships.

Q **Moe Berg, Hank Aaron, Joe DiMaggio, Jackie Robinson, Ted Williams, and Danny Kaye.**

These five players—and Danny Kaye, one-time owner of the Seattle Mariners—were all awarded the Presidential Medal of Freedom.

Q **Alvin Dark, Mike Hargrove, Tommy Helms, Frank Howard, Harvey Kuenn, Pete Rose, Jim LeFebvre, Lou Piniella, Frank Robinson, and Bill Virdon.**

These players were both Rookie of the Year and major league managers.

Q **Ichiro Suziki, Hideo Nomo, Bobby Valentine, Hideki Irabu, Cecil Fielder, Shigetoshi Hasegawa, Kazuhisa Ishii, Tomokazu Ohka, Masanori Murakami, and Alfonso Soriano.**

They all speak Japanese. Fielder learned it when he played in Japan. Soriano, a native of San Pedro De Macoris in the Dominican Republic, played in the Eastern League, the Japanese minors, in 1996. He played for the Hiroshima Tokyo Carp of the Central League in 1997. Valentine became fluent in Japanese when he managed in Japan.

Q **Denny McLain, Mike Sadek, Grover Cleveland Alexander, and Bruce Benedict.**

Each married the same woman twice.

McLain and his wife Sharyn were married, divorced, then remarried. Likewise, Sadek married his wife, Diane. They were later divorced and remarried. (Sadek is probably the only man in the world who owns a baseball autographed by Pope John Paul II.)

Alexander married, divorced, remarried, and redivorced his wife.

Benedict married Kathleen McCormack on October 1, 1979. They divorced in 1983 but remarried in 1986.

Q **Jung Bong, Sang-Hoon Lee, and Tommy Phelps.**

All were born in Seoul, South Korea.

Q **Dave Winfield, Alex Cole, Vince Coleman, Ron LeFlore, and Randall Simon.**
They were all arrested at the ballpark!

On August 4, 1983, Dave Winfield was arrested at Exhibition Stadium in Toronto after a ball he threw in the outfield hit and killed a seagull. He was charged with cruelty to animals and posted $500 bond. The case was dismissed the next day because the incident had been accidental.

On August 9, 2001, former major leaguer Alex Cole was arrested at the Ballpark at Harbor Yard in Bridgeport, Connecticut, home of the Bluefish, an independent team. He was charged by federal authorities with trafficking in drugs. Bail was set at $100,000. After pleading guilty to conspiring to possess heroin with the intent to distribute it, he was sentenced to 18 months in prison.

On July 24, 1993, Vince Coleman (then with the Mets) threw an M-80 firecracker out the window of a car into a crowd in the parking lot at Dodger Stadium in Los Angeles. Three people, including a two-year-old girl, were injured. Coleman was arrested on felony charges, but after entering a plea of guilty to a reduced charge of possessing an explosive device, his sentence of one year in the county jail was suspended. Instead, he was sentence to probation, fined $1,000, and was sentenced to perform 200 hours of community service.

Once one of the most exciting players in the game, Ron LeFlore was at Tigers Stadium on September 24, 1999, to help commemorate the stadium's last night. He was arrested by Wayne County sheriff's deputies on a 1993 warrant for failure to pay child support. LeFlore's daughter had tipped off the police that her father would be at the stadium.

Each of the incidents rates very high on the "bizarre" scale, but the winner in the clubhouse, in our opinion, is the arrest of Randall Simon of the Pittsburgh Pirates at Miller Park in Milwaukee.

As is traditional at Brewers' home games, mascots—dressed as a bratwurst, a Polish sausage, an Italian sausage, and a hot dog—race around the infield warning track.

On July 9, 2003, as the sausage race came perilously close to the visitors' dugout, Simon swung a baseball bat and hit the Italian sausage in the back of the head. Nineteen-year-old Mandy Block, inside the costume, fell and knocked down Veronica Piech, inside the hot dog costume.

Simon was handcuffed and taken to the county jail.

The women suffered only minor scrapes and did not wish to prosecute him. Simon paid a fine of $432 on a charge of disorderly conduct and gave each mascot an autographed bat.

Dishonorable mention: Although not arrested at the ballpark, minor leaguer Jae-Kuk Ryu was arrested for something he did at the ballpark. On April 21, 2003, Ryu, a pitcher with the Dayton Cubs (Class A Advanced Florida State League), threw a number of balls at "Ozzie," a nesting osprey sitting on the perch where he had lived for years on a 40-foot light pole in left field at Jackie Robinson Ballpark. Ryu's final throw hit Ozzie and blinded him in one eye. Ozzie died a few days later. Ryu was charged with harming a protected bird, a misdemeanor. Ryu was later sent down the Class A Lansing Lugnuts (GO NUTS!). He later entered a plea of no contest and was sentenced to perform 100 hours of community service, which he unsuccessfully tried to buy his way out of, by paying $100 per hour. He eventually performed the community service and avoided 60 days in jail.

Q **George Burns, Willie Davis, Jack Fournier, Jeff Heath, Babe Herman, Bob Johnson, Joe Kuhel, Vada Pinson, Tim Raines, Pete Rose, Jimmy Ryan, Juan Samuel, Harry Stovey, Mike Tiernan, Mickey Vernon, and Bill White.**

Each of these players had over 100 career home runs, 100 triples, and 100 doubles. All the other players to reach these lofty heights have bronze plaques on the wall in a building in a small town in upstate New York—or soon will.

Q **Maury Wills, Luis Sojo, Dizzy Trout, Johnny Podres, and Chris Chambliss.**

These players returned to the major leagues after they had played in old-timers' games.

Q **Ray Knight, Brandon Knight, Joe Knight, John Knight, Lon Knight, Gene Kingsale, Sidney Ponson, and Calvin Maduro.**

All are knights. Kingsale, Ponson, and Maduro, all natives of Aruba in the Dutch Antilles, were knighted on April 30, 2002. The ceremony—which Queen Beatrix of the Netherlands was unable to attend—was presided over by governor Olindo Koolman, a devoted baseball fan.

Q **Jimmy Piersall, Pat Deasley, Charlie Faust, Bernie Carbo, Tony Horton, Jack Crooks, Ed Doheny, Pete Browning; and Hall of Famers John Clarkson, Johnny Evers, Rube Foster, and George Davis.**

These major leaguers all spent time in mental institutions.

And this list does not include Brian Looney, Frederick "Crazy" Schmidt, or the Eastern Hospital for the Insane Team of Medical Lake, Washington.

Hall of Famer "Happy" Jack Chesbro worked in the Massachusetts state mental institution, and Orlando "El Duque" Hernandez worked in a psychiatric institution in Cuba.

Q **Joe Judge, Judge Emil Fuchs, Judge Nagle, and Nelson Figueroa.**

They were all "judges." Figueroa played for Brandeis University, home of the "Judges."

Q **Tucker Ashford and Phil Niekro.**

Ashford has one green eye and one brown eye. Niekro has one green eye and one blue eye.

Q **Don Newcombe (1949), Don Schwall (1961), Bill Dawley (1983), Alvin Davis (1984), John Hudek (1994), Hideo Nomo (1995), and Jeff Zimmerman (1999).**

These seven players started the season in the minors and wound up playing in the major league All-Star Game the same year.

Q **Greg Maddux, Todd Dunwoody, Wade Boggs, Larry Walker, Frank Catalanotto, Bernie Williams, Jeff Bagwell, Wally Joyner, Jose Cruz Jr., Troy Percival, Bobby Kielty, Bernard Gilkey, Al Martin, Ben McDonald, Eduardo Perez, and Russ Ortiz.**

They all had LASIK eye surgery.

Q **Jackie Jensen, Ed Sprague Jr., Todd Ziele, Royce Clayton, and Don Drysdale.**

These four major leaguers were married to Olympic athletes.

Jackie Jensen's wife, Zoe Ann Olsen, won a silver medal in springboard diving in 1948 and a bronze in 1952.

Kristen Babb-Sprague won a gold medal in 1992 Summer Olympics in solo synchronized swimming.

Julianne McNamara, Todd Ziele's wife, won silver medals in team gymnastics and floor exercise and a gold medal on the uneven bars at the Los Angeles Olympics in 1984.

Royce Clayton's wife, Samantha Davies, ran the 200 meters for Great Britain in the 2000 games in Sydney, Australia.

Ann Meyers, who was married to Hall of Famer Don Drysdale, played on the American basketball team in the 1976 Montreal Olympics.

Q **Reno Bertoia and Elvis Presley.**

They were born the same day: January 8, 1935.

WHAT'S YOUR HOBBY?

BASEBALL IS AN ART

Drawing cartoons	Ken Griffey Sr.
Ceramics	Buzz Capra
Murals	Buzz Capra
Writing cartoons	Masao Kida
Watercolors	Elrod Hendricks
Mechanical drawing	Paul Lindblad
Painting and drawing	Rawley Eastwick
Landscape and wildlife art	Mike Stanton
Making posters	Stan Perzanowski
Stained glass	Greg Riddoch
Mosaics	Bob Oliver
Pottery	Brad Komminsk
Designing and making jewelry	Jim Bouton

Leathercrafts	Doug Konieczny, Phil Garner, Dave Johnson
Sketching	Joe Ferguson, Don Carman
Painting	Terry Foster

HUNTING, FISHING, AND GOLF

The three most common hobbies listed by ballplayers are hunting, fishing, and golf. But a number of hunters and fishermen are specialists.

Snake hunting	Bob Davis
Raccoon and coyote hunting	Coach Vern Hoscheit
Ice fishing	Wayne Terwilliger
Grouper fishing	Toby Hall
Spear fishing	Chris Snelling
Hunting and fishing in the Everglades	Pat Putnam

WHAT DO YOU READ?

Poetry	Jack McKeon, Don Baylor, Jack Kucek
History	Roberto Clemente
Cowboy history	John Young
Comics	Luis Alvarado, Mike Cuellar, Willie McCovey
Hypnosis	Bob Floyd, Bill Greif
Psychic phenomena	Bill Grief

WORKS WELL WITH ANIMALS

Bird watching	Umpire Ron Luciano
Raising Appaloosas	Coach Gordy McKenzie
Raising horses	Roger Metzger, Roger Craig, John Goryl, Ken Reitz
Cutting horses	Kenny Rogers
Paso Fino horses	Ruben Sierra
Rodeo riding	Ron Clark
Breeding Persian cats	Mike Vail
Rooster fights	Pedro Borbon Sr.
Raising game chickens	Jim Qualls
Training pigeons	Lowell Palmer, Ray Culp Jr.
Tropical fish	Bruce Bochte, Dave Leonhard
Raising dogs	Mike Krukow, Bob Coluccio, Mike Parrott, Peter Hamm, Bob Stickels, Steve Bedrosian
Breeding German shepherds	Ron Guidry, Doug DeCinces, Greg Gross, Tony Cloninger
Training German shepherds as police dogs	Ray Newman
Raising Labrador retrievers	Ken Berry
Raising and training Labrador retrievers for field trials	Steve Waterbury
Training bird dogs	Maury Wills, Tom Bruno, Mike LaCoss
Raising Great Danes	Buddy Schultz
Training hunting dogs	Vic Correll

LET ME SHOW YOU MY COLLECTION DEPARTMENT

Bobblehead dolls (including his own)
Antique trucks
Classic cars
Rocks and shells
Rocks
Brass collectibles
Baseball cards

Baseball memorabilia
Autographs of baseball Hall of Famers in
    his copy of the *Baseball Encyclopedia*
Baseballs signed by other relief pitchers
Knives
Guns

Antique clocks
Watches
World Wars I and II memorabilia
Indian artifacts
Footwear

Steve Cox
Gary Redus
Reggie Jackson, Jack Clark, Al Holland
Chet Lemon
Jerry Tabb
Denny Walling
Mark Ryal, Chris Richard, Doug Linton, Brian
    Edmondson, Tom Pagnozzi
Joe Kerrigan
Ron Gardenhire

Troy Percival
Umpires Rich Garcia and Dale Ford
Umpires Rich Garcia and Dale Ford, Jim Rooker,
    Chuck Hockenbery
Mike McCormick
Jesse Levis
Umpire Bob Engel
Rick Bladt
R. J. Reynolds

Coins	Bruce Kison, Ed Crosby, Bob Priddy, Rusty Staub, Tom Tischinski, Joe McIntosh, Buddy Schultz, Tom Shopay, Gene Michael, Ed Ott, Lowell Palmer, Carl Taylor, Buddy Schultz
Stamps	Bruce Kison, Tom Bradley, Darryl Evans, Chris Short, Rusty Staub, Rick Henninger, Chuck Hockenbery, Lowell Palmer, Rick Sweet, Forrest "Spook" Jacobs[1]

BEST OF THE REST

Cliff diving	Joe Wallis
Writing letters to former major leaguers	Jerry Dipito
Making lamps out of broken bats	Coach Mark Cresse
Yoga	Preston Lee Hanna
Pantomime	Dennis Lamp
Logging	Rich Rodas
Cleaning cars	Wayne Gomes
Square dancing	Hy Cohen
Working with plastics	Reggie Smith
Astrology	George Theodore
Astronomy	John Denny, Butch Wynegar, Gary Rajsich
Rock climbing	Umpire Jim Reynolds

Anthropology	George Theodore
Oceanography	Pete LaCock
Arm wrestling	Ken Harrelson
Farming	Steve Bedrosian
Growing desert plants	Coach Joe Sparks
Jai alai	Coach Tony Pacheco
Airplane mechanics	Johnny Sain
Model planes	Galen Cisco, Ozzie Virgil, Jack Krol, Mike Caldwell
Canoeing	Mike Stanton
Writing lyrics	Ross Baumgarten
Mountain climbing	Jim Beattie
Playing Scrabble	Glenn Adams
Building things	Jim "Catfish" Hunter
Watching cartoons	Bob Lacy
Building model ships	John Denny
Firearms	Umpire Joe West
Ham radio	Barry Bonnell
Air hockey	Glenn Burke
Fly tying	Jim Kern
Dancing	Al Chambers, Mike Felder, Luis Delgado, Art Gardner, Pat Kelly, Larry Johnson, Gary Mathews, J. R. Richard, Eddie Solomon, Rennie Stennett

Singing	Dwight Smith, Johnny Bench, Bobby Bonds, Thad Bosley, Morris Madden, Tim Foli, Myron White, Derrell Thomas, Manny Sarmiento, Rick Waits, Roy Lee Jackson, Lamar Jackson, Lee Maye, Dwight Smith
Corresponding	Al Bumbry
Searching fields with a metal detector	Ruppert Jones
Listening to soft music	Edgardo Romero
Geology	Greg Erardi
Practical jokes	Larry Andersen
Juggling	Darrin Fletcher
Hapikido karate	Jim Gott
Kite flying	Ty Van Burkleo
Trapping	Tom Henke, Eugene Matt Brabender, Rick Auerbach, Larry Gura, Russ Snyder, Rich McKinney
Ice skating	Umpire Jim Honochick, Kevin Hickey, Pete Reiser
Speed skating	Lee Mazzilli
Spelunking	Mike Duvall
Building miniature racing cars	Clay Kirby
Badminton	Merv Rettenmund
Television and radio repair	Jerry Dybzinski

Gunsmithing	Jim Kern
Wood splitting	Umpire Terry Tata
Mat surfing	Jim Strickland
Growing roses and desert plants	Coach Joe Sparks
Woodcutting	Umpire Dutch Rennert
Wood carving	Sandy Vance
Magic	Umpires Ed Montague and Al Clark, Larry Walker, coach Wendell Kim
	Umpire Ed Runge
Driving Baja Bugs (a cross between a Volkswagen Beetle and a dune buggy)	
Dune buggy racing	Mark Ballanger
Toy trains	Umpire Jerry Crawford, Ike Brown, Chris Christensen
Archery	Umpire Bill Hohn, Dave Watkins, Mac McNertney, Jody Davis, Reid Nichols, Larry Gura, Chuck Goggin
Snowshoeing	Umpire Jim Reynolds
Locksmithing	Bryan Hass
Wine making	Umpire Ed Rapuano
Taxidermy	Ned Yost, Rick Auerbach, Benny Edelen, Steve Waterbury
Rocketry	Jim Willoughby

Sightseeing

Assembling toys

Greek mythology

Darts

Jigsaw puzzles

Electricity

JFK assassination research

Christmas lighting

Refurbishing vintage Porsches

Orlando Peña

Terry Whitfield

Chet Lemon

Tom Brookens

Johnny Hairston

Tom Hilgendorf

Umpire Terry Craft

Umpire Jim Joyce

Umpire Tim Timmons

Note

1. On October 1, 2001, the National Baseball Hall of Fame and Museum in Cooperstown opened a special exhibit of the Spook Jacobs's baseball stamp collection. His collection of over 500 stamps, from 36 countries and spanning over 70 years, is said to represent 80 percent of all the baseball stamps ever issued around the world. Included are variations, errors, rarities, autographs, first-day covers, and unique postmarks, as well as the first baseball stamp ever issued (Philippines, 1934).

15

WHERE ARE YOU FROM?

Q **Name a Romulan who played in the majors.**
Charlie Lau, from Romulus, Michigan.

Q **What's the connection: Keith McDonald, Craig House, Dave Roberts, Stephen Randolph.**
All were born in Japan.

Q **Name a big leaguer who went to high school in Rome.**
Archi Cianfrocco. He went to high school in his native Rome, New York.

Q **Name a Haligonian who played in the majors.**
Rick Lisi, a native of Halifax, Nova Scotia.

Q **Who was the best Wilrijkian in the majors?**
Brian Lesher. He's a native of Wilrijk, Belgium.
   What—another *story about a guy from Wilrijk?*

Q **Name an Aiean in the majors.**

Benny Agbayani, who lives in Aiea, Hawaii.

> **BALLPLAYERS WHOSE HOMETOWNS YOU CANNOT PRONOUNCE CORRECTLY THE FIRST TIME DEPARTMENT**

Tlalnepantla, Mexico, birthplace of Rodrigo Lopez. Edo Anzoategui, Venezuela, hometown of Giovanni Carrara. Kwangsan-Ku Songjungdong, South Korea, birthplace of Byung-Hyun Kim.

Q **"I'm a big leaguer. In the off-season, I live in Europe. Who am I?"**

Ralph Milliard, a native of Curacao. In the winter, he lives in Amsterdam.

Tigers prospect Shane Heams went from Temperance (Ohio) Bedford High School to Champagne College.

Q **Name a Liverpudlian in the majors.**

John Johnstone, a native of Liverpool, New York.

Q **Name a native of Vienna who played in the big leagues.**

Kal Daniels, born in Vienna, Georgia.

Q **Name a Dry Pronger in the majors.**

Alan Newman, who lives in Dry Prong, California.

Q **Scouts should have known early on that Len Barker would be a money player. Why?**
He's from Ft. Knox, Kentucky.

The 1998 Reds media guide notes this about general manager Jim Bowden: "A Weston, MA, and Boothbay Harbor, ME, native, Jim was born May 18, 1961."
   Sorry, you can only be a native of one place.

Q **Name a Kabulian in the majors.**
Jeff Bronkey (1993–1995, Texas Rangers, Milwaukee Brewers), a native of Kabul, Afghanistan.

PLACES WE WISH WERE BALLPLAYERS' HOMETOWNS DEPARTMENT

Yankee, Colorado; Yankee, New Mexico; Tigers Valley, Ohio; Giants Neck, Connecticut; Cardinal, Virginia; Mariner, Maine; Dodger Point, Washington; Rangers Landing, Kentucky; Marlin, Pennsylvania; the Rockies, Washington; Angel, Alabama; Padres Mesa, Arizona; Oriole, Maryland; Blue Jay, West Virginia; Heavenly Twins, Montana; Little Twins, Colorado; the Twins, Alaska; Twins Mine, Arizona; Indians Hills, Utah; Reds Place, Colorado; Pirate Cove, Oregon; Brewers, Georgia; Pilots Cove, Washington.

Q **What's the connection: George Chalmers, Dave Abercrombie, Tom Waddell, Hugh Nicol, Mike Hopkins, Mike McCormick, Jim McCormick, Mac MacArthur, John Connor.**
Like Bobby Thomson, they're all from Scotland.

IT'S EASY TO REMEMBER WHERE PRESTON GOMEZ IS FROM DEPARTMENT

Q **Where was Preston Gomez born?**

Preston, Cuba.

Q **Where is Fred Cambria from?**

Cambria Heights, New York.

Q **Name a Wailukuian in the majors.**

Shane Victorino. He's from Wailuku, Hawaii.

Q **Who is the most modest player in the game?**

Nate Bland, a resident of Humble, Texas.

Q **Jackie Robinson was the first major leaguer from Cairo, Georgia. Who is the second?**

Willie Harris.

Q **Name a major league umpire who lives in Poland.**

John Hirschbeck lives in Poland, Ohio.

16

WHO AM I?

Q **"My name is Jesus. I was born on Christmas Day. I played in the major leagues. Who am I?"**
Jesus Manuel Trillo, born December 25, 1950, in Maracaibo, Venezuela.

Q **"Through 2003, there has never been a major leaguer whose last name starts with the letter X. I am the first man to homer off pitchers whose last names start with all the other 25 letters. Who am I?"**
Jim Thome.

Were you going to say Babe Ruth? Sorry. He never homered off a pitcher whose last name started with I.

Q **"One year, I finished third in the league in the home run championship race. I was also third on my team in home runs. I'm the only player who can make this claim. Who am I?"**
Tony Lazzeri. In 1927, Lazzeri's 18 home runs made him third—a very distant third—in the American League and on the New York Yankees. Babe Ruth was first with 60, and Lou Gehrig was second with 47.

The year 1927 was the only year since 1900 in which teammates finished first, second, and third in the home run race in either league.

Q **"I pitched to Ted Williams and Darryl Strawberry. Who am I?"**

Jim "Kitty" Kaat. He broke in with the first Washington Senators team in 1959. Kaat pitched through 1983, Strawberry's first year in the majors.

Q **"I won 20 games in each of my first four full seasons—the only pitcher since 1900 to do so. I am *not* a Hall of Famer. Who am I?"**

Wes Ferrell. Between 1929 and 1932, he won 21, 25, 22, and 23 games, respectively, for the Cleveland Indians.

Q **"On October 1, 1961, Roger Maris broke Babe Ruth's record for most home runs in a single season when he hit his 61st home run of the season. I was Maris's teammate that year. On April 8, 1974, Hank Aaron broke Ruth's record for most home runs in a career when Aaron hit home run #715. I was on the field for that game. Who am I?"**

Al Downing. In 1961, he was a teammate of Roger Maris. By 1974, Downing was pitching for the Los Angeles Dodgers and gave up Aaron's historic blast.

Q **"I managed a minor league team to a league championship. The next year, I played in a big league game. Who am I?"**

Luis Sojo. In 2002, Sojo managed the Norwich Navigators, then affiliated with the New York Yankees, to the championship of the Class AA Eastern League.

On September 6, 2003, Sojo was back in Yankee pinstripes and had an at-bat against the Boston Red Sox at Yankee Stadium.

No, he was not booed as he walked to the plate. That was the sound of 55,000 fans shouting "Luuuuuuuis!" Thanks to Ed Randall for this story.

Q **"I pitched in three World Series for three different teams in three different decades. Who am I?"**
Billy Pierce: Detroit Tigers, 1945; Chicago White Sox, 1959; San Francisco Giants, 1962.

Q **"I pitched in 73 consecutive games that my team won—the major league record. Who am I?"**
John Smoltz, Atlanta Braves: June 3, 2002–May 25, 2003.

Q **"I am the only man to homer in 23 consecutive seasons *for the same team*. Who am I?"**
Carl Yastrzemski, Boston Red Sox, 1961–1983.

Q **"I was the Most Valuable Player in my league in my first full season in the league. Fifteen years later, I was thrown out of the last game I ever played in the majors. Who am I?"**
Vida Blue. Although he pitched briefly for the Oakland A's in 1969 and 1970, 1971 was his first full season and he won the American League MVP Award, going 24–8 with an ERA of 1.82.

On October 2, 1986, Blue, then pitching for the San Francisco Giants, was ejected by home plate umpire Greg Bobin in the sixth inning of a 2–1 Giants loss to the Houston Astros. Blue had argued balls and strikes with Bonin. Blue never pitched again.

But he did return to the Candlestick Park mound on September 24, 1989, for a much happier occasion. It was not to throw out a ceremonial first pitch. Why was Blue back on the mound?

To get married! How many people can say, "I got married at my old office"?

Q **"On Sunday, September 14, 2003, I made my big league debut by pinch-hitting for my brother. Who am I?"**
Mike Glavine, New York Mets, who pinch-hit for his brother Tom.

Q **"I am the only pitcher to start All-Star Games 15 years apart. Who am I?"**

Roger Clemens. His first start in the All-Star Game was in 1986. He started again in 2001.

Q **"I was a teammate of Paul Waner and Tug McGraw. Who am I?"**

Warren Spahn. He teamed with Waner on the 1942 Boston Braves and with McGraw on the 1965 New York Mets.

Q **"I was born in Butzbach, Germany, and went to school in Paris. I'm a big leaguer. Who am I?"**

Ron Gardenhire. He attended Paris Junior College in Paris, Texas.

Q **"I was born in Zeeland and went to college in Holland. I'm a big leaguer. Who am I?"**

Jim Kaat. A native of Zeeland, Michigan, he attended Hope College in Holland, Michigan.

Q **"I broadcast the first National League game in Canada. I also broadcast the first American League game in Canada. Who am I?"**

Harry Caray. On April 14, 1969, Caray was behind the microphone for the St. Louis Cardinals as they opened the Expos' first season in Montreal at Jarry Park.

On April 7, 1977, Caray was back in Canada, broadcasting for the Chicago White Sox as they opened the Blue Jays' first season at Toronto's Exhibition Stadium.

The Cardinals lost their game. So did the White Sox.

Q **"I'm the first man to hit home runs for three different teams in the World Series. Who am I?"**

Matt Williams: San Francisco Giants, 1989; Cleveland Indians, 1997; Arizona Diamondbacks 2001.

Q **"One year, I led the league in grounding into double plays, strikeouts, and errors. Nevertheless, I was selected as the Most Valuable Player. Who am I?"**

Joe Gordon. In 1942, he led all American Leaguers in grounding into double plays (7), strikeouts (95), and errors (28), but he hit .322 and led his New York Yankees to the American League championship.

Q **"I was a teammate of Harmon Killebrew and Tony Gwynn. Who am I?"**

Graig Nettles. He was a teammate of Killebrew on the Minnesota Twins, 1967–1969. Later, he was on the San Diego Padres with Tony Gwynn, 1984–1986.

Q **"I'm a big leaguer. I used to be the Phillies bat boy. Who am I?"**

Ruben Amaro Jr.

Q **"I'm a Hall of Famer. The high school I went to was on the site later occupied by Atlanta-Fulton County Stadium. Who am I?"**

Luke Appling.

Q **"In four separate seasons, I hit at least 30 home runs before the All-Star Game. Who am I?"**

Mark McGwire. In 1987, he hit 33 before the break, on his way to his rookie record 49. In 1997, he had 31 home runs before the midseason classic and another 27 after it. In his historic 1998 season, McGwire hit 37 homers before the All-Star Game and another 33 after it. He hit 30 homers before the break in 2000 but only 2 afterward.

Q "For three consecutive years, I hit over 40 home runs and had more homers than strikeouts. I am *not* a Hall of Famer. Who am I?"

Ted Kluszewski, Cincinnati Reds: 1953, 40 home runs, 34 strikeouts; 1954, 49 home runs, 35 strikeouts; 1955, 47 home runs, 40 strikeouts.

Q "I'm the team doctor for a major league team. My grandfather was president of the United States. Who am I?"

Warren G. Harding III, MD, team doctor for the Cincinnati Reds, 1987–1989.

Q "I'm a big leaguer. My daughter was the first in vitro fertilization baby born in America through normal delivery. Who am I?"

Mike Flanagan. On July 9, 1982, Kathy Flanagan gave birth to Kerry Ellen.

Q "I was the first college basketball player to score at least 1,000 points in a season. Later, I played in the major leagues. Who am I?"

For the 1951–1952 season at the University of Seattle—where he teamed with his twin brother, Eddie, who also played in the majors—Johnny O'Brien scored 1,051 points in just 37 games. He later played for the Cardinals, the Pirates, and the Braves.

Q "I was with the New York Yankees on May 14, 1967, when Mickey Mantle hit his 500th home run. I was with the Braves on April 8, 1974, when Hank Aaron hit his historic 715th home run in Atlanta. Who am I?"

Frank Tepedino.

Q **"I was a big leaguer. My son is a major league umpire. Who am I?"**

Ed Montague Sr. His son is Ed Jr.

 Jeff Kunkle also played in the majors. His father, Bill, was a major leaguer and a big league umpire.

Q **"I'm a big leaguer. My parents were voted 'Worst Little League Parents in History' in Hartford, Connecticut. Who am I?"**

Rob Dibble.

Q **"One year, I played for the team that set the American League record for most wins in a single season. Eight years later, I played for the team that set the National League record for most losses in a single season. Who am I?"**

Joe Ginsberg. He was with the 1954 Cleveland Indians, who won a record 111 games. He was also with the 1962 Mets, who lost a record 140 games.

Q **"I'm a big leaguer. John Elway was the best man at my wedding. Who am I?"**

Mike Aldrete. He and Elway were roommates at Stanford.

Q **"I'm a big league manager. During my playing career, I caught three no-hitters including a perfect game. My daughter-in-law was the 1998 national bodybuilding champion. Who am I?"**

Jeff Torborg. He caught Sandy Koufax's perfect game. His son Dale, who wrestles professionally as "The Demon," is married to Christie Wolf, a former Hawaiian Tropic bikini model. She wrestles professionally as "Asya."

Q **"Even though my professional baseball career consisted of just two minor league games, Hollywood made a movie about me. Who am I?"**

A lifelong baseball fan, Harry Ruby played in one game for the Hollywood Stars in 1935, when he was 40, and another for the Los Angeles Angels in 1940—both times, the team's final game of the season. In the 1935 game, Ruby batted against another lifelong baseball fan—actor and occasional minor league umpire Joe E. Brown— who pitched for the San Diego Missions. Ruby wrote such songs as "Baby Face," "Three Little Words," "Who's Sorry Now?" "I Want to Be Loved by You," and "Hooray for Captain Spaulding." Richard Bernard "Red" Skelton played Ruby in the 1950 biography *Three Little Words*.

Q **"I was the first man to hit two postseason walk-off home runs. Who am I?"**

Bernie Williams, New York Yankees. On October 9, 1996, in Game 1 of the American League Championship Series, Williams homered in the bottom of the 11th inning off Randy Myers to give New York a win against the Baltimore Orioles.

He did it again on October 13, 1999, in the bottom of the 10th inning in Game 1 of the American League Championship Series off Rod Beck to seal a 4–3 Yankees victory over the Boston Red Sox.

I Didn't Know That

Q **Why were baseball exccutives firing guns into the ground on January 3, 1962?**
As part of the groundbreaking ceremonies for the Astrodome in Houston, Colt .45s were shot into the ground to mark the future home of the Colt .45s, later the Houston Astros.

Q **How many players have hit at least 35 homers and driven in at least 100 runs in 8 consecutive seasons?**
Only 3 so far:
    Sammy Sosa, Chicago Cubs, 1995–2003
    Jimmie Foxx, Philadelphia Athletics, Boston Red Sox, 1932–1940
    Rafael Palmeiro, Baltimore Orioles, Texas Rangers, 1995–2003

Q **000010000000100000001000000**
This is not a binary code. What is it?
Nolan Ryan's home run totals, year-by-year, 1966–1993. Ryan holds the modern record for most seasons in a career in which he hit no more than one home run—27.

Q **Which major league stadiums are the closest to each other?**
U.S. Cellular Field and Wrigley Field in Chicago are just 9.81 miles apart.

Q **"I was a major league manager. Seven men who played for me were big league managers in 2001. Who am I, and who are they?"**
The mentor to the seven big league managers listed below, with the teams they managed, is Hall of Famer Tommy Lasorda of the Los Angeles Dodgers.

Davey Lopes (Brewers), Mike Scioscia (Angels), Phil Garner (Tigers), Jeff Torborg (Expos), Bobby Valentine (Mets), Dusty Baker (Giants), Johnny Oates (Rangers).

Q **Name three Jewish graduates of Los Angeles's Fairfax High School who played in the 1959 World Series.**
Larry Sherry and Norm Sherry of the Los Angeles Dodgers and Barry Latman of the Chicago White Sox.

In 1980, Jack Perconte and his family were involved in a gunfight in Two Guns, Arizona. They helped capture a suspect.

The ballistic incident did not involve Marge Schott, Paul Derringer, Scott Winchester, Lee Smith and Barry Wesson, Carl Furillo "The Reading Rifle," or Jimmy Winn "The Toy Cannon."

Q **Name a big leaguer who was a Bandit.**
Homer Bush. In 1993, he played in Australia for the Brisbane Bandits.

Chris Chambliss's baby-sitter was Arlene Helney, later Mrs. Elston Howard.

Aaron Small is 6'5" tall.

José Pagan is a member of the Fellowship of Christian Athletes.

Q **Why did Twins first baseman David Ortiz leave the game against the Kansas City Royals on April 8, 2000?** Hint: He was not injured and was neither pinch-hit nor pinch-run for nor was he replaced for defensive purposes.

Ortiz was replaced because a throw from Twins third baseman Corey Koskie broke the pocket of Ortiz's first baseman's mitt. Ortiz wears his mitt on his right hand. He was the only left-handed first baseman on the Twins, and he had only one mitt.

FOR THIS I WAITED 21 YEARS? DEPARTMENT

Q **Who went the longest between big league hits?**
Charlie O'Leary. He broke in with the Tigers in 1904 and went to the Cardinals in 1913. He was out of the majors until 1934, when he came to bat once for the St. Louis Browns. O'Leary waited NINE YEARS for one game, one at-bat, one hit, one run scored.

Q **Name a major leaguer whose wife was a professional football player.**
Danny Frisella. His wife Pamela was an offensive end on an all-female professional football team in Detroit.

Cal McLish weighed 12 pounds at birth.

THIS DAY IN BASEBALL HISTORY DEPARTMENT

Q **On July 28, 2000, Bob Wickman was traded from the Milwaukee Brewers to the Cleveland Indians. What was the promotion on July 29 at Milwaukee's County Stadium?**

"Bob Wickman Poster Night." The Brewers gave out 30,000 posters of the player they had just traded.

Q **How did Florida Marlins outfielder Mark Smith hit two home runs and get a save on the same day?**

On July 2, 2000, Smith's two home runs helped the Marlins beat the Expos 2–1 in Montreal. The day was already memorable for Smith, as it was his first two-homer game. The Marlins then flew to Miami, and Smith, accompanied by teammate Brad Penny, was driving from the airport in Ft. Lauderdale on I-75 when they saw a car swerve over a highway median strip and onto a grassy knoll. The car was smoking by the time Smith and Penny arrived and, with another Good Samaritan, kicked out the glass in the back window. Just minutes before the car exploded, Smith reached into the back seat and yanked the sole occupant out of the car, saving his life.

For his heroism, Smith was given the 2001 Steve Palermo Award by the Baseball Assistance Team (BAT).

Q **Was June 12, 2000, a good day or a bad day for Bobby Jones of the Mets?**

Both. On that date, the Mets sent right-handed pitcher Bobby J. Jones down to their AAA farm club in Norfolk, Virginia. To fill his roster spot, they called up left-handed pitcher Bobby M. Jones.

Q **Why did Mark McGwire decline an invitation to be with President Bill Clinton as he delivered the State of the Union address on January 19, 1999, before a joint session of Congress?**

Because he was taping an episode of *The Simpsons*. D'oh! The episode, "Brother's Little Helper," was first broadcast on October 3, 1999.

A set of 20 stamps honoring baseball legends was released on May 12, 2000. Although individual players have been on U.S. stamps before, these were the first issued as a set. Those honored are Jackie Robinson (his second stamp), Eddie Collins, Christy Mathewson, Ty Cobb, George Sisler, Rogers Hornsby, Mickey Cochrane, Babe Ruth (his third stamp), Walter Johnson, Roberto Clemente (his second stamp), Lefty Grove, Tris Speaker, Cy Young, Jimmie Foxx, Pie Traynor, Satchel Paige, Honus Wagner, Josh Gibson, Dizzy Dean, and Lou Gehrig (his second stamp).

Hank Aaron was at the ceremony unveiling the stamps in Atlanta, where he was joined by relatives of 15 of the players depicted, including Roberto Clemente Jr., Josh Gibson Jr., Rogers Hornsby III, and Rogers Hornsby IV. 225 million stamps in the set were printed.

Q Who is the most obscure ballplayer ever to appear on an American postage stamp?

Frank "Wildfire" Schulte, who was the model for the image on a stamp issued February 3, 1998, commemorating the first World Series of 1903.

Q Why did Cleon Jones bat right and throw left?

The ballfield where he learned to play in Mobile was configured in such a way that it was easier for him to hit with power as a right-hander.

Q Why did Mickey Lolich throw left-handed?

A fall off his tricycle when he was three broke his collarbone. His doctor recommended special exercises for his left hand.

Q **When a member of the Milwaukee Brewers hits for the cycle, he literally hits for the cycle. Why?**

Whenever a Brewer hits for the cycle at home, Harley Davidson, whose corporate headquarters is in Milwaukee, presents him with one of its new motorcycles.

When *former* Brewer Jose Valentin hit for the cycle as a member of the Chicago White Sox on April 28, 2000, a teammate presented him with a toy motorcycle.

Q **In 1970, Bobby Bonds of the Giants set a major league record by striking out 189 times. Whose record did he break?**

His own. In 1969, he fanned 187 times.

John Franco always wears an orange undershirt in tribute to his late father Jim who was a New York City sanitation worker. Orange was part of his uniform.

TRICK QUESTION DEPARTMENT

Q **Honus Wager blamed an umpire for the death of his best friend, Jason Weatherbee. Why?**

Jason Weatherbee was Honus Wagner's dog, a fixture on the Pirates' bench at home games for nine years. Wagner claimed that the dog understood baseball. In a game in May 1912, Wagner was ejected for arguing with umpire Clarence "Brick" Owens. As Wagner left the game to return to the dugout, Jason dashed out of the dugout and bit the umpire's leg. (The umpire claimed that Wagner sicced the dog on him.) Wagner said Jason "never seemed well after he went up against Umpire Owens that day. I shouldn't wonder if he got hold of the umpire's leg and that poisoned him."

Q Many fans deride umpires by shouting, "You're blind, ump!", or "Hey, ump—you're missing a great game!" Which major league umpire really *was* blind?

Hall of Fame umpire Nestor Chylak. During his military service during World War II, he was blinded for 10 days by an exploding German artillery shell.

Q On May 17, 2000, Cal Ripken Jr. tied one of Hank Aaron's career records, but wished he hadn't. Which one?

Grounding into the most double plays in a career. In an 8–7 loss to the Angels that day, Ripken grounded into a double play for the 328th time in his career, tying Aaron's record. By the end of his 21-year career, Ripken had grounded into a total of 350 twin killings, a record likely to remain unchallenged for years.

Q Ballplayers are always changing—bats, pregame rituals, food, batting stances, t-shirts, socks, mental approaches, anything to give them an edge, particularly at the plate.
Name a major leaguer who changed his face during a game.

Luis Sojo. On October 1, 2001, playing at home for the New York Yankees, Sojo came to bat in the second inning looking like he had all year—with a moustache. But when he came to bat again in the third inning, the moustache was gone. He had shaved it between at-bats, thus helping the Yankees beat the White Sox 8–1.

Q Name a major leaguer (and later a broadcaster) who was a member of the Royal Canadian Mounted Police—the Mounties.

Jean-Pierre Roy.

Q On October 4, 2001, at San Diego's Qualcomm Park, after he scored the 2,246th run of his career—more than anybody else in the history of baseball—teammates presented Rickey Henderson of the Padres with a gold-plated home plate. But that was not enough for Henderson. What did he do four days later?

He went back to Qualcomm, and with the assistance of the grounds crew, he dug up and "stole" home plate.

Q The New York Yankees did it during a visit to the Boston Red Sox at Fenway Park on April 22, 1922—the first team ever to do so. What did they do?

The Yankees wore uniform numbers on their road uniforms.

Q Just when we thought the wacky-clubhouse-stunt trophy had been retired by Sparky Lyle, who had a penchant for dropping his pants and sitting, nude, on clubhouse birthday cakes, along comes Jay Buhner and his "special" talent. What is it?

Mr. Buhner, the pride of Louisville, Kentucky, had the ability—the unique ability, as far as we can tell—to vomit on cue.

Q How did Bo Belinsky meet his second wife, Jane Weyerhauser?

She was drowning off a beach in Hawaii when Belinsky rescued her.

Q How did Rich Pharris, who is a player but not a baseball player, get Tulsa Drillers manager Tim Ireland ejected from an April 21, 2002, game against the Arkansas Travelers?

Pharris is the organist at Ray Winder Field at War Memorial Park in Little Rock, home of the AA Texas League Travelers. He played music between batters rather than between innings, and it annoyed Ireland who complained to the umpires, got into an argument, and was ejected. As Ireland walked off the field, Pharris played "Happy Trails."

GUYS WE REALLY SHOULD INTRODUCE DEPARTMENT

Randy Keisler, who went on the disabled list in May 2002 after he was bitten on his pinky by a pygmy rattlesnake on his Tampa property, we'd like you to meet Bob Davis. His hobby is snake hunting.

TRICK QUESTION DEPARTMENT

Q **Which minor league team plays at Fifth Third Field, named for the Midwest giant Fifth Third Bank?**
There are three correct answers. The Toledo Mud Hens, the West Michigan White Caps, and the Dayton Dragons all play in parks with the same name: Fifth Third Field. (Okay, Fifth Third Ballpark for the White Caps in Comstock Park.)

JUST A PHONE CALL AWAY DEPARTMENT

Q **Which major league club is closest to its AAA affiliate?**
Hint: Four affiliates are within 100 miles of their big league clubs.

Oakland–Sacramento? At 81 miles, a good guess. But not the closest.

How about Denver–Colorado Springs? Again, at 69 miles, another good guess, but also wrong.

Then it must be Boston and Pawtucket, just 44 miles apart. You could probably drive that between innings. No, none of those is the correct answer.

The major league team whose AAA affiliate is the closest is the Seattle Mariners. Their top farm club, the Tacoma Rainiers, is only 35 miles away.

Q **Which major league club was farthest from its AAA affiliate?**

From 1965 to 1967, the AAA affiliate of the Washington Senators was the Hawaii Islanders, a mere 4,834 miles away. Yes, it was just a phone call away, but a $95.30 phone call!

Q **On April 6, 2002, Jesse Orosco did something he had not done since 1984. What did he do?**

He scored a run.

Q **Opening Day, April 12, 1965, was a memorable day for Jim Kaat and the Minnesota Twins, as they hosted the Yankees in Minneapolis. Besides the fact that he was the Opening Day starter, what made it memorable for Kaat?**

He got to the game at Metropolitan Stadium by helicopter. As Kaat told us exclusively, "The Minnesota River had flooded over. I was driving to the stadium. Traffic backed up. Got out and asked the guy ahead of me what the problem was. When he told me, I returned home and called WCCO radio, which broadcasts our games. They sent their traffic helicopter out to Burnsville High School, picked us up in the parking lot, and took us in two at a time: Rich Rollins, Dick Stigman, Bill Bethea, and me. Only 16,000 in attendance. Had the game won 4–3 with two outs in the ninth, man on second. Joe Pepitone hits a little pop-up to Cesar Tovar at third. He dropped it!!!! I was already to shake hands with catcher Earl Battey. Tovar felt so bad. He singled in the winning run in the 11th. I did not figure in the 5–4 decision. It bonded a great friendship between Cesar and me."

(Bethea was a victim of bad luck. After a 10-game cup of coffee in 1964, Bethea was back in spring training with the Twins in 1965. He was told that he had made the team, and he sent his wife and baby north to Minneapolis with all of their belongings. She drove from Orlando pulling a trailer. On Opening Day, the team made a move, acquired a veteran player and he was optioned back to Charlotte. So Bethea was there physically on Opening Day, but not active.)

Thanks to Jim Kaat for this great story.

Q **Frank Pastore once did something in nine and a half minutes which most people cannot do at all. What did he do?**

He ate a 72-ounce steak at Amarillo's Big Texas steakhouse.

Q **Only five pairs of teammates have combined for at least 100 home runs in a single season. Who are they?**

Mickey Mantle (54) and Roger Maris (61), 1961 New York Yankees—115.

Barry Bonds (73) and Rich Aurilia (37), 2001 San Francisco Giants—110.

Babe Ruth (60) and Lou Gehrig (47), 1927 New York Yankees—107.

Mark McGwire (70) and Ray Lankford (31), 1998 St. Louis Cardinals—101.

Alex Rodriguez (57) and Rafael Palmeiro (43), 2002 Texas Rangers—100.

Q **These teams finished in precisely the same order—1, 2, 3, 4, 5—in their division for five yeas in a row. Which teams and which division?**

The division is the American League East. The teams, and the order 1996–2002

New York Yankees

Boston Red Sox

Toronto Blue Jays

Baltimore Orioles

Tampa Bay Devil Rays

This is the only time that five teams have finished in the same order in their division (or in their league) even *twice* in consecutive years.

Q **Only two men played in the post-season every year there was a postseason (i.e., not 1994) from 1991 to 2002. Who are they?**

Tom Glavine and Mike Stanton.

Glavine's games were all with the Atlanta Braves.

Stanton's teams in the post-season were Atlanta (1991, 1992, 1993), Boston (1995), Texas (1996), and the New York Yankees (1997, 1998, 1999, 2000, 2001, 2002.)

Q **When was the last time that the highest-paid player in baseball was on a World Champion team?**

1986: Gary Carter. His salary was $2,160,714 for the Mets.

Q **When Rickey Henderson of the Boston Red Sox hit his first home run of the season on April 27, 2002, he tied the record for homering in the most consecutive years, 24. Whose record did he tie?**

Ty Cobb. Henderson's historic homer also extended his exclusive record for most lead-off home runs in a career to 80. Henderson also homered in 2003 for the Los Angeles Dodgers—to make 25 years.

Q **Four other men homered in 23 consecutive seasons. Three are Hall of Famers: Hank Aaron, Carlton Fisk, and Carl Yastrzemski. Who is the fourth?**

Rusty Staub.

Umpire John Shulock's favorite food is elk sausage.

Julio Franco of the Atlanta Braves went to Divine Providence High School in San Pedro de Macoris in the Dominican Republic. When he comes to bat, the music he asks the soundboard operator at Turner Field to play is "God Is in Control" by Twila Paris.

Q Who was Matt Kinney's Little League coach in Bangor, Maine?

Stephen King. *"Now listen, guys. At the count of three, we're all going to stare at their pitcher. We'll make him EXPLODE!"*

Q Which professional ballpark has the best address?

Pringle Park, home of the West Tennessee Diamond Jaxx, in the Class AA Southern League. The park is at #4 Fun Place, Jackson, Tennessee.

III

POSTSEASON

GET A JOB

Many ballplayers, coaches, executives, and umpires have second jobs, either before they became ballplayers, during the off-season, or when their baseball careers were over. Here are some we thought were unusual.

Grain elevator operator	Mike Bordick
Oil truck driver	Umpire Jerry Crawford
Waterman	Keith Atherton
Surgical supplies dealer	Bill Almon
Car-leasing business	John Candelaria
Private detective	Moose Haas
Nightclub performer	Nellie Briles
Bricklayer	Tom Henke
Motorcycle shop owner	Lou Piniella
Mortuary worker	Ty Gainey
Pipe fitter	Logan Easley
Marina owner	Boog Powell

Marine salvage	Rudy May
Hair studio owner	Umpire Nick Bremigan
Window-cleaning business	Frank Malzone
Florist	Joe Lefebvre
Boxing instructor	Umpire Larry Napp
Owner, limousine service	Umpire Jim Evans
Venezuelan soap opera star	Ozzie Guillen
Film extra	Ray Lamb
Co-owner of 15 pizzerias	Ernie Whitt
Cosmetics firm owner	Sam McDowell (*What, "Suddenly you are beautiful!"?*)
Police officer	Bill Kunkel
Deputy sheriff	Umpire Satch Davidson
Probation officer	Duff Brumley, Ken Suarez
Juvenile probation officer	Ed Vargo
Animator for Walt Disney	Bobby Pfeil
Special police officer	Umpire Nick Colosi
Owner of a nine-hole golf course	Bill Mazeroski
Billiards parlor owner	Sam McDowell
Greeter	John Costello (worked at Whitey Herzog's restaurant)
Evergreen salesman and distributor	John Ellis
Accountant	Jamie Cocanower
Rest home operator	Buddy Bradford

Furniture salesman	Jim Rittwage
Mariners clubhouse attendant	Tom Lampkin
Golf store owner	Butch Henry
Owner, Caribbean Embroidery Company	Edgar Martinez
Rock singer	Scott Radinsky
Movie stand-in for Gene Hackman	Greg Goossen[1]
Model	Stan Bahnsen
Travel agent	Dal Maxvill
Actuary	Tony Brizzolara
Professional pool player	Deron Johnson
Wholesale hardware dealer	Ted Uhlaender
Investment broker	Lou Piniella
Stock broker	Tom Runnels
Owner, oil and gas drilling company	Dave Geisel
Stuntman	Paul Ratliff
Realtor	Felipe Crespo, Paul Schaal
Basketball referee	Jeff Manto
Paint business	Umpire Ted Hendry
Mexican garden urn salesman	Allen McDill
Barber, barbershop owner	Ramon Ortiz
Fumigator	Gavvy Cravath
Typesetter	Nap Rucker

Mule seller	Zack Wheat
Hotelier	Vic Willis
Tarping cotton modules	Brooks Kieschnick
High school wrestling coach	Steve Kline
Cartoonist	Robert Cremins
Milkman	Buck Weaver
Sand blaster	Steve Cox
Coalminer	Stan Coveleski
Bouncer	Rick White
Welder	Willie Hernandez
Plumber	Geno Petralli
Driving instructor	Keith Hernandez
"Jet hoist" distributor	Steve Hargan
Roughneck (oil rig worker in the North Sea)	Doug Ault
Dentist	Steve Arlin
Juice salesman	Jim Perry
Lumber salesman	Joe Lis, Bill Singer
Lumberjack	Jim Obradovich
"Physical development machinery" salesman	Stan Thomas
Owner, carpet-cleaning business	Tom House
Cement-mixer driver	Larry Cox

Police officer	Bob Oliver
High school biology and science teacher	Bruce Dal Canton
Pecan business	Bill Russell and his partner Jim Brewer
President of an escrow company	Don Sutton

WHAT DO YOU FARM?

Ostrich	Brett Butler
Chicken	Claude Osteen
Catfish (10,000 head)	Umpire Larry McCoy
Tobacco	Woodie Fryman
Dairy business operator	"Milkman" Jim Turner

Note

1. Thanks to Gene Hackman to alerting us about this one.

THE EDUCATED BALLPLAYER

Q **Name a big leaguer who won a high school varsity letter in curling.**

Reggie Cleveland: Cardinals, Red Sox, Rangers, Brewers (1969–1981). Cleveland is a native of Swift Current, Saskatchewan. Curling is one of Canada's two national sports. Cleveland won a varsity letter at Cold Lake High School in the other one, too—hockey.

Danny Goodwin has a Bachelor of Science Degree in Zoology from Southern University.

Al Holland is the proud owner of a Bachelor of Science Degree in Recreation from North Carolina A & T University. Perhaps he'd like to chat with Ray Burris who earned his B.A. from Southwestern State in Weatherford Oklahoma, in the field of Recreational Leadership. Carl Willis's degree from the University of North Carolina at Wilmington is in Park and Recreation Management. Go Seahawks!

Bryan Clark majored in Dental Hygiene at Fresno City College.

Jim Cox has a Bachelor of Science degree in microbiology from the University of Iowa.

Q **Name a big leaguer who did postgraduate work at the University of Edinburgh in Scotland.**

Jim Colburn, not to be confused with Mark Mercer, who attended Pan American University in Edinburg, Texas.

Q **Name a big league manager who studied at Oxford.**

Don Kessinger, who earned a Bachelor of Science degree in business administration from the University of Mississippi, in Oxford, Mississippi.

AWARDS

Ballplayers, managers, coaches, writers, executives, and umpires have been honored in many ways. Their numbers can be retired; they can be elected to the Baseball Hall of Fame in Cooperstown or to other halls of fame; they can have stadiums, streets, or ballfields named for them.

Another way they can be honored is by having awards named for them.

Since 1981, the Associated Press sports editors have presented the Red Smith Award for sports writing.

Thomas A. Yawkey bought the Boston Red Sox in 1933 and owned the team until his death in 1976. The Sox established their own most valuable player award, and since 1937, it has been called the Thomas A. Yawkey Memorial Award.

The first Roland A. Hemond Award was presented, appropriately, to Roland A. Hemond during the 31st annual convention of the Society for American Baseball Research in July 2001 in Milwaukee. Hemond has been an executive with the Orioles, White Sox, Angels, and Diamondbacks. The award commends Hemond for his long support for scouts.

The Mel Ott Award is given each year to the National League home run champion.

The Texas Rangers Wives Association won the Jim Sundberg Community Service Award in 1990—surely one of the few times any major league baseball award was not won by a man.

The Bill Slocum Award, named for the great sportswriter, is presented for service to baseball.

The Carl Yastrzemski Award is given annually to the best high school player in Suffolk, New York. The award is given by the Suffolk County Baseball Coaches' Association. The best pitcher in the county gets the Paul Gibson Award.

The St. Louis Chapter of the Baseball Writers Association of America presents an annual Bob Bauman Physical Comeback Award.

The San Francisco Giants have created only one award named for a player—the Willie Mac Award, established in 1980 and presented to the Giant player who best "exemplifies the leadership and spirit shown by Willie McCovey."

Each year since 1988, the Giants have also presented the Harry S. Jordan Award to the spring training player who, in the opinion of all the other players in camp, best exemplifies the Giants' spirit. Jordan was a long-time minor league trainer with the Giants.

The Milton Richman Memorial Award, given by the Association of Professional Baseball Players of America since 1989, is presented to the person who has given the most of his time and effort to promote the mission of the association, which is to assist present and former ballplayers who are in need.

The association also gives the Win Clark Award each year. It is presented to the first year player from the Southern California area who had the most outstanding season. First given in 1951 to Lee Walls, the award has been presented to Jim Lefebvre, Willie Davis, Johnny Callison, Mike Epstein, Willie Crawford, Joe Moeller, Tim Wallach, Mark Grace, Jeff Cirillo, and Tony Gwynn, among others.

Thanks to Dick Beverage of the association for this information.

The Roberto Clemente Man of the Year Award began in 1970 as the Commissioner's Award, given annually to the player who best exemplifies the game, sportsmanship, community involvement, and the individual's contribution to his team. Following Clemente's untimely death on New Year's Eve 1972 in a plane crash while bringing relief supplies to earthquake-ravaged Managua, Nicaragua, the award was renamed in Clemente's honor. John Hancock Financial Services now sponsors the award and presents it during the World Series with a check for $25,000 to the recipient's favorite charity.

The Gordon Cobbledick Tomahawk Award, named for the Hall of Fame writer, has been given to a member of the Cleveland Indians by vote of the players since 1963. It is given to the player who makes the biggest contribution to the team.

An annual scholarship at Cleveland State University is named for Luke Easter.

AWARDS

Major League Baseball gives the "21" Award in honor of Roberto Clemente.

Kinston, North Carolina, presents an annual Lewis B. McAvery Award for outstanding contributions to professional baseball. Lewis McAvery was the stadium superintendent at Grainger Stadium for over 25 years.

The Milo Hamilton Community Service Award is presented by the RBI Foundation of Houston. Hamilton won the Ford C. Frick Award—the highest award in baseball broadcasting—at the Hall of Fame in 1992. Hamilton broadcast for the Browns, Cardinals, Cubs, White Sox, Pirates, and Astros.

The Seattle Mariners have given the Ellis Award since 1998 to recognize community involvement by a Mariners' minor-leaguer. The award is named for John Ellis, chairman emeritus of the team.

The Baseball Alumni Team (BAT), which helps retired ballplayers, presents an annual Bart Giamatti Caring Award, named for the late commissioner of baseball. BAT also gives a Steve Palermo Award for bravery and courage, named for the former umpire who was shot and permanently disabled trying to break up a robbery.

Hillerich and Bradsby has presented a Silver Bat each year since 1949 to the batting champions in each league. Since 1946 (when the award was still given to minor leaguers), each winner also gets the John A. "Bud" Hillerich Memorial Award.

The Dick Howser Award, named for the late manager of the Kansas City Royals, has been given annually since 1987 to the outstanding member of the Royals' player development department.

Q **Football's annual award to the nation's top college defensive back is named after a mediocre baseball player. Who and why?**

Although Jim Thorpe hit only .252 in his six-year big league career with the Giants, Reds, and Braves, his accomplishments on the college and professional football gridirons were legendary. He helped popularize both college and professional football and was the first commissioner of what became the National Football League. A statue of Thorpe sits at the entrance to the Pro Football Hall of Fame in Canton, Ohio.

The Lou Boudreau Award is given to the best minor league position player in the Indians organization.

The University of Minnesota gives an annual Dave Winfield Award to its best pitcher. Winfield pitched during his college career there.

The Ewing M. Kauffman Award, named for the late owner of the Royals, has been given annually since 1970 to the outstanding member of the Royals' scouting department.

The Cy Young Award, presented annually since 1956 (the year after Young died), is given to the outstanding pitcher in each league. From 1956 to 1966, one award was given. Starting in 1967, each league has had its own Cy Young Award winner.

The Jackie Robinson Rookie of the Year Award was originally called the J. Louis Comiskey Award, named for the son of White Sox owner Charles Comiskey, who inherited the team when his father died. The name of the award was changed in 1987. It is now presented annually by the Baseball Writers Association of America. Robinson won the first award in 1947. Starting in 1949, a separate award has been given in each league.

The Lou Brock Base-Stealing Championship Award—the first major award named after an active player—has been given annually since 1978 to the National League's most prolific base stealer.

The San Diego Padres have named an annual award for Clyde McCullough, who spent nearly 50 years in baseball. He was a coach for the Padres in 1982. Originally given to their best rookie, the award has been given since 1990 to the Padres' best pitcher.

The Dave Stewart Community Service Award has been given annually since 1996 by the Oakland A's to the member of the team who has done the most for the community. Stewart pitched for the A's from 1986 to 1992 and briefly in 1995.

The Ford C. Frick Award, given annually by the Baseball Hall of Fame in Cooperstown, has gone to an outstanding broadcaster since 1978.

The Robert O. Fishel Award is given annually for excellence in the field of public relations to the "active, nonuniformed representative of Major League Baseball whose ethics, character, dedication, service, professionalism, and humanitarianism best represent the standards propounded by Robert O. Fishel." Fishel was an executive with the Browns, Indians, and Yankees and later the American League. The plaque listing annual winners is displayed in the Hall of Fame museum.

The Warren Giles Award has been given annually since 1984 by Minor League Baseball to the outstanding president of a minor or summer league. Giles, a Hall of Famer, was president of the National League, 1951–1969.

The Larry MacPhail Trophy, named for the innovative Hall of Fame executive, has been presented annually since 1966 to a minor league club for outstanding promotion.

The Bob Freitas Award has been given each year since 1989 by the National Association, the governing body of the minor leagues, at a lunch during the winter meetings to an outstanding minor league organization. Freitas worked in minor league baseball for over 20 years, helping owners old and new with innovative promotions.

The Gene Autry Courage Award has been presented annually since 1994 to people in sports whose "life and actions demonstrated special courage in the face of challenge." Sammy Sosa was the first major leaguer to win it. Umpire Steve Palermo was also given the award. See www.tempe.gov/govrel/pastrecip.htm.

The Milton Richman "You Gotta Have Heart" Award is presented annually by the Baseball Writers Association of America. The award is named for the Hall of Fame writer.

The Jack Butterfield Player of the Month Award, instituted by the Yankees shortly after Butterfield's death in 1979, was named for the team's vice president of player development and scouting.

The Elston Howard Player of the Week Award, also instituted by the Yankees in 1979, is named for the Yankee catcher and coach who died in 1980. Howard was the first African American man to play for the Yankees. A catcher and an outfielder, Howard was an All-Star from 1957 to 1965 and was the American League's Most Valuable Player in 1963. The Yankées retired Howard's number (32) and erected a plaque to him in Monument Park at Yankee Stadium.

The James P. Dawson Award has been presented almost annually since 1956 by the Yankees to the outstanding rookie in spring training. Dawson was a sportswriter for the *New York Times* who died during spring training while covering the Yankees.

The Lou Gehrig Award has been given annually by Gehrig's Columbia University fraternity Phi Delta Theta since 1955 to the big leaguer who best exemplifies Gehrig's giving character. See www.phideltatheta.org/news.asp?id=111&mypage=0.

Each year since 1972, the New York Mets have presented the John J. Murphy Award to their outstanding rookie in spring training. In 2000, the award went to Garth Brooks, who had worked out with the team in camp. The Mets were impressed with his spirit and charity work.

Murphy was the Mets' general manager in 1969 and helped mold the team into world champions. When he was a major league pitcher (Yankees, Red Sox, 1932–1946), he helped the players' union get the teams to provide meal money for all players. Murphy passed away in 1970, a beloved part of baseball's rich lore.

Notre Dame University gives an annual award named for Hall of Fame sportswriter Wendell Smith.

The Branch Rickey Award has been presented annually since 1991 by Major League Baseball to a player for outstanding community service.

The Jack Krol Award is given each year by the San Diego Padres since 1994 to honor an outstanding contributor in the team's player development office. Krol was a Padres coach from 1981 to 1986.

Each year since 1980, the Anaheim Angels have given the Fred Haney Memorial Award to the outstanding Angel rookie in spring training.

The Warren Spahn Award was first presented in 1999. The winner was Randy Johnson of the Arizona Diamondbacks, who was presented with a bronze statue of Spahn by Warren Spahn himself in Guthrie, Oklahoma, where Spahn lives. The award is given to the majors' best left-handed pitcher.

The Montreal Expos have given an annual John Michael Award since 1988 to their outstanding minor league staff member, in honor of their former president, general manager, and chief executive officer.

Since 1898, the Expos have also presented an annual Charles Bronfman Award (named for their first owner) for excellence in scouting.

Each year since 1977, the Milwaukee Brewers have given the Harvey Kuenn Batting Award, named for their former manager (1982–1983), to their top hitter.

Gorman Thomas is, so far, the only man to win the Milwaukee Brewers Hank Aaron Home Run King Award. Thomas won it in 1979, when he led the American League with 45 homers, and again in 1982 with 39.

The Hank Aaron Award was first presented in 1999 by Major League Baseball to the top hitters in each league, based on the league leaders in RBIs, hits, plus home runs. Starting in 2000, the award has been presented by a panel of broadcasters.

The Maryland Professional Baseball Players Association presents an annual Jack Dunn Memorial Service Award, usually to an Oriole. Dunn was an executive with the Orioles.

The Marlins give the Carl Barger Player Development Person of the Year Award, named for their late first president.

The Garry Maddox Award is presented by the Philadelphia Child Guidance Center.

The Hutch Award is named for Fred Hutchinson, a pitcher and later the manager of the Cincinnati Reds. He was diagnosed with cancer in 1963. The Hutch Award has been given annually since 1964 to the major leaguer who best shows Hutch's character, fighting spirit, and competitive desire. For a complete history of the award, see www.baseball-almanac.com/awards/aw_hut.shtml.

Each year since 1992, the Colorado Rockies have awarded the Doug Million Minor League Rockie of the Year Award to their outstanding minor leaguer.

The Baltimore Orioles give the Elrod Hendricks Award, named for their longtime player and coach, for Oriole community service.

The Genc Autry Award (not to be confused with the Gene Autry Courage Award) has been given by the Angels since 1961 to the team's most valuable player. It is voted on by teammates.

The Cleveland Indians give an annual Bob Feller Award to their best minor leaguer pitcher in his first season in professional baseball.

The annual Most Valuable Oriole Award is named for Lou Hatter, a sportswriter who covered the Orioles for 27 years. It has been presented by the Sports Boosters of Maryland since 1954, when the Orioles returned to the major leagues.

The Thurman Munson Award is given each year to the player with the highest batting average in the Cape Cod League.

The pitcher who strikes out the most batters in the American Legion annual competition gets the Bob Feller Award.

The Joan Payson Award for community service is given annually by the New York chapter of the Baseball Writers Association of America. It is named for Joan Whitney Payson, the first owner of the New York Mets.

The Jim Boyer Memorial Award is presented each year to the Western Maryland College (Westminster) baseball student-athlete who "best emulates Boyer's qualities of loyalty to Western Maryland, commitment to athletic and academic excellence, and genuine care for others." Boyer was an American League umpire from 1944 to 1950.

Major league players themselves decide on the Players' Choice Marvin Miller Man of the Year Award, given annually to the player who has contributed to his community in a way that inspires others to higher levels of achievement. Marvin Miller was the executive director of the Major League Players Association and helped mold the union into the most successful, most powerful union in the history of the labor movement. During his tenure (1966–1982) the players earned arbitration, free agency, and many other rights. During that time, the players' average salary went from $19,000 to $240,000.

Dale Berra won the Stedler Award for the 1975 Niagara Falls Pirates in the short season Class A New York–Penn League presented by the league's official scorers to the player likely to "go the furthest in baseball."

The Fred Hofmann Memorial Award, named for the player and former Orioles scout who died in 1964, has been given annually since 1965 to a member of the Orioles scouting and player development staff.

The Kenny Myers Memorial Award is given each year since 1972 by the Angels to the team's best minor-leaguer. Myers was a scout and hitting instructor with the Angels.

The Tony Conigliaro Award has been given annually by the Baseball Writers Association of America to those in baseball who have overcome adversity with spirit, determination, and courage.

Tony Conigliaro was one of the brightest stars in baseball during his brief career with the Red Sox. In 1965, he hit 32 home runs. His career was, for all practical purposes, ended on August 18, 1967, when he was hit in the left eye by a pitched ball. Although he rebounded somewhat in 1969, when he hit 20 homers, he never really recovered and died in 1990—just 45 years old.

Since 2002, the Jenkins Cup has been presented to the winner of the Canadian Baseball League. It is named for the league's first commissioner, Ferguson Jenkins, a member of both the American and the Canadian baseball halls of fame.

The Fred Sington Trophy is presented annually to the top athlete from Alabama.

The Baseball Writers Association of America gives an annual Judge Emil Fuchs Award for long and meritorious service to baseball. Fuchs was the owner of the Boston Braves.

The Negro Leagues Baseball Museum in Kansas City presents an annual Oscar Charleston Award.

UNBREAKABLE RECORDS

0

Number of fans with paid admission at a major league game. After the devastating strike by major league players in 1994, teams tried to win back fans with a variety of promotions. On May 12, 1995, the Astros distributed free tickets to their game against the Phillies. Those who had already purchased tickets were given vouchers good for tickets at a future game.

Number of home games won by the New York Mets in the month of August 2002. They lost all 13 games at Shea Stadium. No other National League team has ever gone winless in a month at home.

Number of assists in a game by an entire team: Mets over Philadelphia 5–1, June 25, 1989, 13 strikeouts, 12 fly-outs, two groundballs to first base.

Q **Two teams have won the World Series three times in seasons in which they had zero grand slams. Which teams?**

The Boston Red Sox in 1915, 1916, and 1918 and the Los Angeles Dodgers in 1959, 1965, and 1981.

The Washington Senators reached this tyable but unbreakable record in 1924, when they won their only World Championship. The 2003 Florida Marlins are the most recent team to achieve this dubious distinction.

2

Number of players who hit four home runs in a single game in the same season. Mike Cameron of the Seattle Mariners smacked four four-baggers on May 3, 2002. Three weeks later, Shawn Green of the Los Angeles Dodgers duplicated that feat on May 23, 2002, adding a single and a double on his way to a National-League-record 19 total bases in the game.

Q **Since 1900, only one man has managed two American League teams in the same city. Who is he?**

Joe Gordon: Kansas City Athletics (1961), Kansas City Royals (1969).

To break this "record," a manager would have to skipper three *American League teams in the same city. Seems unlikely, no?*

3 + 3

On April 9, 2000, in the sixth inning, Ron Coomer, Jacque Jones, and Matt LeCroy hit consecutive home runs for the Minnesota Twins. In the very next inning, Carlos Beltran, Jermaine Dye, and Mike Sweeney hit consecutive home runs for the Kansas City Royals. This was the first time that opposing teams had ever hit three consecutive homers in the same game. It was also the first day in big league history in which any two teams—opponents or not—hit three consecutive home runs.

4

Number of times Twins pitcher Mike Trombley has been in uniform when another player in the game got his 3,000th hit. Three were by teammates. He gave up the other one.

Trombley was a Twin on September 16, 1993, when teammate Dave Winfield got hit #3,000. On June 30, 1995, Trombley, still with the Twins, gave up Eddie Murray's 3,000th hit. On September 16, 1996—exactly three years after Winfield's hit—Twins teammate Paul Molitor got his 3,000th. Trombley was a reliever with the Orioles on April 15, 2000, when teammate Cal Ripken Jr. got his 3,000th hit. (After that hit, a single, Ripken was greeted at first base by Orioles first-base coach Eddie Murray.)

Number of managers fired in April 2002—the first full month of the season: Buddy Bell (Colorado Rockies), Davey Lopes (Milwaukee Brewers), Phil Garner (Detroit Tigers), and Tony Musser (Kansas City Royals).

Most batting titles in a career by a man who is not in the Hall of Fame and won't be: Bill Madlock—1975 Cubs, .354; 1976 Cubs, .339; 1978 Pirates, .341; 1983 Pirates, .323. Every eligible player ahead of him or tied with him is a Hall of Famer, and the rest will be: Ty Cobb (12 batting titles); Tony Gwynn and Honus Wagner (8); Rod Carew, Rogers Hornsby, and Stan Musial (7), Ted Williams (6); Wade Boggs (5); Roberto Clemente, Harry Heilmann, Cap Anson, and Dan Brouthers (all tied with Madlock at 4).

6

Number of home runs hit by six different players on one team in one modern game, on April 9, 2000, by J. D. Drew, Shawon Dunston, Edgar Renteria, Jim Edmonds, Craig Paquette, and Mark McGwire of the St. Louis Cardinals.

7

Number of managers Dock Ellis played for in a single big league season. Billy Martin was his first manager with the New York Yankees when the 1977 season opened. In April, Ellis was traded to Oakland, managed by Jack McKeon. McKeon was soon replaced by Bobby Winkles. When Ellis was sold to the Texas Rangers, his manager was Frank Lucchesi, who was then replaced by Eddie Stanky. Stanky quit after just one game. His replacement as Rangers manager was Connie Ryan. Ryan didn't last long either—just six games. His successor was Billy Hunter.

8

Number of colleges attended by one major leaguer, Skip Lockwood: Merrimack, Boston College, Bryant & Stratton, Marquette, Carroll, Emerson (BS in speech), Fairfield (masters in business and industrial communication), and Columbia (doctorate in sports psychology).

12

Number of major league teams played for by pitcher Mike Morgan: Oakland A's, New York Yankees, Toronto Blue Jays, Seattle Mariners, Baltimore Orioles, Los Angeles Dodgers, Chicago Cubs, St. Louis Cardinals, Cincinnati Reds, Minnesota Twins, Texas Rangers, Arizona Diamondbacks.

17

Mel Ott led the New York Giants in home runs in all 17 seasons between 1928 and 1945.

Most consecutive seasons with a home run by a pitcher—Warren Spahn, 1948–1964.

18

Number of years between Nolan Ryan's first no-hitter—July 15, 1973, a 6–0 win for the Angels over the Tigers—and his last (and seventh), May 1, 1991, a 3–0 win for the Texas Rangers over the Toronto Blue Jays.

Most World Series umpired—Bill Klem.

23

Number of consecutive seasons batting over .300—Ty Cobb.

24

Number of years in the major leagues by one man before getting into his first World Series—Mike Morgan. He broke into the majors in 1978 but did not reach the Series until 2001 with the Arizona Diamondbacks.

26

Most World Championships won by a single team—the New York Yankees. In fact, even if you combine the number of championships won by any American city's teams in other professional sports—baseball, hockey, football, basketball—nobody beats the Yankees.

28

Fewest games played at a position by a Gold Glove winner. In 1999, Rafael Palmeiro was voted a Gold Glove at first base, even though as a result of injuries, he played only 28 games there for the Texas Rangers—28 games!

42

Number of major league baseball stadiums homered in by Fred McGriff.

89

Travis Phelps was drafted by the Devil Rays in the 89th round of the 1996 draft—the lowest-drafted player ever to make it to the majors. He made his major league debut with Tampa Bay on April 19, 2001. In 1998, the number of rounds in the draft was reduced to 50, making Phelps's record unbreakable.

100

Q **Who is the first pitcher to win 100 games at Fenway Park?**
Roger Clemens. On August 31, 2003, Roger Clemens, then with the Yankees, won #100. He also recorded 55 losses there.

108

Most World Series games umpired—Bill Klem.

110

Number of postseason games (through 2004) announced by Bob Sheppard, the public address announcer at Yankee Stadium since 1951.

369.02

Number of innings pitched by Walter Johnson for the 1916 Washington Senators without surrendering a home run. Eighty-six years after it was set, this remains the modern record.

391+

With his 661st home run on April 13, 2004—which put him ahead of Willie Mays and at #3 on the all-time home run list—Barry Bonds had homered off a record 391 different pitchers. Every time Bonds homers off a pitcher for the first time, he breaks his own record.

Hank Aaron homered off 310 pitchers, Willie Mays off 267, and Babe Ruth connected off a mere 216 pitchers.

10,328

Most outs made in a career at the plate plus on the bases: Pete Rose. He's the only player with 10,000 outs.

WHICH RING DO YOU WEAR?

Eighty-five rings were ordered for the players, coaches, manager, trainers, and executives with the World Champion 2003 Florida Marlins. Ugueth Urbina's was specially sized to fit on his thumb. Designed by team owner Jeffrey Loria himself, the rings include 228 white diamonds, 13 rubies, and a Belgian teal diamond for the eye of a marlin. Each ring weighs a quarter of a pound and includes the player's uniform number and name.

Through our travels in the baseball world, we've met lots of people—players, retired players, scouts, broadcasters, executives, and so forth—who have been awarded championship rings of one sort or another. Some have earned more than one.

So we thought we'd ask—"Which ring do you wear?" Here are some of the interesting answers.

When **Jim Kaat** retired in 1984 after a 25-year pitching career, he had pitched in the majors longer than anyone. He went on to be a pitching coach with the Reds and a broadcaster with the Twins (1988–1993) and New York Yankees (1986, 1995–).

The only ring he wears is the 1982 St. Louis Cardinals World Championship ring. Why? As Kaat told us, "It's the only one I earned."

"Nice of the Yankees to give me rings and the Twins of '91 [for his role as broadcaster], but I had nothing to do with those teams' success."

Jim Bouton: "When I wear my ring, which isn't often, it's the '63 [American] League Championship ring. It's more colorful than the '62 [Yankees] World Championship ring. The '63 ring has the Yankee top hat with rubies and sapphires, as opposed to the single diamond in the '62 ring. Also, I feel that I contributed to the '63 ring [his record was 21–7 in 249.3 innings with an ERA of 2.53] whereas in '62 I mostly sat on the bench and cheered [7–7, 133 innings, 3.99 ERA]. And I learned never to pass my ring around the table anymore at a sports dinner. One time it came back as an SMU class ring. Everybody got a big laugh, but I haven't done it since."

Red Sox broadcaster **Joe Castiglione** wears his 1986 American League Championship ring with great pride. That team came within one strike of winning the World Series. Now he also wears his 2004 Red Sox World Championship ring.

Tommy Hutton, Florida Marlins broadcaster: "The only ring I wear occasionally is the 1997 Marlins World Championship ring. As a broadcaster, the club gave us the exact same ring as the players. The only ring I ever received as a player was our PCL [AAA Pacific Coast League] championship ring from the 1970 Spokane Indians."

Murray Cook, former minor leaguer; Pirates executive; general manager for the Yankees, Expos, Reds; national crosschecker for the 1997 Marlins; and currently a scout with the Boston Red Sox: "I mix them up but mostly wear the Marlins ring from '97. I have given my '79 Pirates ring to my daughter and only occasionally wear the

'71 Pirate one. I sure was looking forward to the 2003 Boston ring. No real reason for wearing the Marlin ring other than it is the latest one earned." Except for the 2004 Red Sox World Championship ring.

Marty Appel, author of numerous baseball books and former publicity director for the New York Yankees: "Although I was given a 1976 World Series ring [the Yankees lost to the Reds] through the generosity of Mr. Steinbrenner, I never wear it; it resides with great pride in a safe deposit box. My feeling is that the rings can be worn by players, enjoyed by others connected with the team. I used to think that the day I wore it, I would run into Ernie Banks and feel terrible [Ernie Banks: 19 seasons, 512 home runs, 0 World Series appearances]. So, it's happily in a bank vault."

Marty Appel told us that he was in charge of ordering the rings for the team in 1978. His own ring fit inside Jim "Catfish" Hunter's size 13½ ring.

Boston Red Sox broadcaster **Jerry Trupiano** wears a championship ring from the 1974 Houston Aeros of the World Hockey Association and the 2004 World Championship Red Sox.

Richard Bresciani, vice president for publications and public relations for the Boston Red Sox: "I mostly wear my 1999 All-Star ring since I was the Red Sox coordinator for the five-day event. However, I sometimes still wear the 1986 American League championship ring, but an arthritic knuckle problem makes it difficult for me to get it on and off. It is an excellent ring, and I'm sorry I don't wear it much anymore. For over 10 years, I wore it all the time. I have my 1975 American League championship ring put safely away." We hope his 2004 Red Sox World Championship ring fits better.

Bobby Murcer, a Yankee broadcaster since 1984, told us that he doesn't wear any rings.

Herb Carneal has been with the Minnesota Twins since they moved from Washington, D.C., in 1961. He has World Championship rings from the Twins triumphs in 1987 and 1991 and another from the 1965 American League Champion Twins. He told us that in 1996, as he was waiting to be introduced as the winner of the Ford C. Frick Award for baseball broadcasting at the Hall of Fame in Cooperstown, he felt a tap on his shoulder. He turned around to see Frank Robinson. Robinson was holding one of Carneal's rings—the only one Carneal had worn that day. Robinson held up the ring and asked, "Does this belong to you?" The ring had slipped off Carneal's finger and fallen to the ground.

Veteran scout and former big leaguer **Tom "T-Bone" Giordano** told us that he has an assortment of rings, including those from the American League Champion Cleveland Indians of 1995 and 1997, the World Champion Baltimore Orioles of 1983, and the American League Champion Orioles of 1979. He told us that which ring he wears depends on his mood.

Former major leaguer **Deacon Jones**, now an advance scout for the Baltimore Orioles, told us that he wears his 1984 National League Champion San Diego Padres ring. Jones was the hitting instructor for the Padres.

Jeff Torborg wears two rings—one on each hand. One is from the 1965 World Champion Los Angeles Dodgers, for whom he played. The other is from the 1981 American League Champion New York Yankees, for whom Torborg was the bullpen coach.

Torborg told us that when he wears the Yankee ring, he wears it on his left ring finger with his wedding ring. The Dodger ring goes on the right pinkie. It was originally sized for his right ring finger, but after Torborg broke that finger, the ring would no longer fit over his knuckle.

RETIRED NUMBERS

Q **As a tribute to Jackie Robinson, on April 15, 1977, the fiftieth anniversary of his big league debut, baseball retired #42 for all teams. But those 14 players who were wearing it on that date were allowed to continue to wear it until the end of their careers. Who is the last #42 in the major leagues?**
Mariano Rivera of the New York Yankees. When Rivera retires, no other player will ever wear #42.

The San Diego Padres have retired #19 for Tony Gwynn.

The A's retired #9 for Reggie Jackson.

The New York Yankees retired #49 on Ron Guidry Day, August 23, 2003.

The Cubs retired #10 for Ron Santo.

On October 7, 2001, at Camden Yards in Baltimore, just before the last game of his career, the Baltimore Orioles retired #8 for Cal Ripken Jr.—while he was still technically active.

The Houston Astros have retired #49 in honor of their former manager and broadcaster Larry Dierker.

Shortly after the June 19, 2002, death of Jack Buck, the longtime broadcaster for the St. Louis Cardinals, the team put up a small pennant next to their other retired numbers at Busch Stadium. It said "Jack" and included his famous catchphrase "That's a winner!"

RETIRED BY A MINOR LEAGUE TEAM

On July 6, 2002, the Lynchburg (Virginia) Hillcats of the Class A Advanced Carolina League retired #26 in honor of their longtime pitching coach, former major leaguer Jim Bibby. It was also "Jim Bibby Bobblehead Doll Night" at Merritt Hutchinson Stadium.

RETIRED BY A COLLEGE

Wright State University has retired #34 for Brian Anderson.

Jamie Moyer's uniform #10 was the first number retired by St. Joseph's College in Pennsylvania.

McClennan Community College in Waco, Texas, has retired Pat Listach's #8.

Valdosta State University in Georgia has had one player who had a cup of coffee in the majors. Sam Bowen played for the Boston Red Sox in parts of two seasons in the early eighties. He wore #14 while a Blazer (1973 and 1974), and that number has been retired.

Oklahoma State University retired baseball uniform #21 in honor of Robin Ventura.

RETIRED BY A HIGH SCHOOL

Los Angeles's Lincoln High School retired #14 for Robert Castillo.

In 1999, California's Bell High School retired uniform #9 in honor of its alumnus Marvin Bernard.

On April 4, 2000, Moreno Valley (California) High School retired #14 in honor of one of its alumni who made it to the majors—Troy Percival.

Harmon Killbrew's Payette, Idaho, high school retired #12 for his prowess as a football quarterback.
   Thanks to Harmon Killebrew and Tim Wiles for this unusual story.

Curt Schilling's number #19 was retired by his high school, Shadow Mountain High in Arizona.

Warren Morris's #13 was retired by his alma mater, Bolton High School, in Alexandria, Louisiana.

The first graduate of Gretna (Virginia) High School to have his uniform number (#7) retired is Tony Womack.

Cardinal Newman High School in Columbia, South Carolina, retired #10 in honor of Ken Vining.

Mets general manager Omar Minaya had his uniform #21 retired by Newtown High School in Queens, New York.

Lafayette High School in Lafayette, Louisiana, retired #6 in honor of Paul Bako—its first graduate to play in the majors.

24

STUFF NAMED AFTER BALLPLAYERS AND OTHERS

Starting in 2002, the most valuable player in the All-Star Game has been awarded the Ted Williams Trophy. The trophy used to be named for Arch Ward, the Chicago sportswriter who created the All-Star Game.

In 2003, the press box at Detroit's Comerica Field was renamed the "Ernie Harwell Media Center." Harwell retired after the 2002 season as the voice of the Tigers.

There's a Manny Mota Little League in his native San Pedro de Macoris, Dominican Republic.

On June 4, 2002, New York City renamed a public school the Mickey Mantle School.

Sandy Alomar Jr. has created a steak sauce.

The press box at Dodger Stadium was renamed for Vin Scully on April 20, 2001. That date marks the anniversary of Scully's first home-game broadcast for the Dodgers (then in Brooklyn), in 1950. The press box will also include a "Wall of Fame," honoring broadcasters and sportswriters who have covered the Dodgers and are members of the Baseball Hall of Fame's broadcasters and writers wings—winners, respectively, of the J. G. Taylor Spink Award for writing and the Ford C. Frick Award for broadcasting. Those so honored are Jaime Jarrin, the Dodgers' Spanish-language broadcaster, and writers Bob Hunter, Jim Murray, and Ross Newhan.

Stan Javier was named for Stan Musial, a teammate of Stan's father, Julian, when he was with the Cardinals, 1960–1963.

The Goose Gossage Baseball Field is in Goose's native town, Colorado Springs.

The press box at Denver's Coors Field was named for the Rockies' first official scorer, Frank Haraway.

"Benny Bean coffee" is a blend from Hawaii's Kimo Bean brand, named for Benny Agbayani.

On August 31, 2000, a historical marker was unveiled and dedicated to Eddie Plank near his birthplace in Gettysburg, Pennsylvania, on the 125th anniversary of his birth.

An official Pennsylvania State Historical Marker was placed at 236 E. Lamb Street, the boyhood home of John Montgomery Ward in Bellefonte on September 16, 2000, close to John Montgomery Ward Field. Eric Milton (who, like Ward, threw a perfect game by age 23) grew up nearby.

The playing field in the Astoria, Queens, section of New York City where Whitey Ford played as a boy has been renamed for him.

Nashua, New Hampshire, has named streets for Don Newcome and Roy Campanella. The streets were dedicated in their names by Rachel Robinson, Jackie's widow, in 1997. Newcome and Campanella played for the Dodgers' Nashua farm club in 1946.

Tony Gwynn Stadium is the new home of the San Diego State Aztecs.

As a part-owner of the Aberdeen, Maryland, Ironbirds, Cal Ripken Jr. has donated $9 million dollars to the construction of Cal Ripken Jr. Stadium.

Twenty thousand small models of the Harry Caray statue outside Wrigley Field are for sale at Harry Caray's Restaurant in Chicago.

A statue to Hall of Famer Max Carey is planned for his native town, Terre Haute, Indiana.

Sammy Sosa was given a star on Calle Ocho on "Sammy Sosa Day" in Miami. He was the first baseball player to have a star embedded on the street where prominent Hispanics are honored.

Schools are named for Jackie Robinson in Chicago, Long Beach (California), Milwaukee, New Haven, and Brooklyn.

There's a Ring Lardner school in Niles, Michigan, his hometown. Lardner received the J. G. Taylor Spink Award in 1963.

A statute of Dodger Hall of Famer Pee Wee Reese, a Kentucky native, was unveiled at Louisville's Slugger Field, home of the RiverBats (the Brewers' affiliate in the AAA International League) on June 29, 2000. Reese's widow Dottie was present. The bronze statue shows Reese, the Dodgers shortstop, making the throw to first base on October 4, 1955, to bring Brooklyn their only World Championship.

There's a Roberto Clemente School in North Philadelphia, Newark (New Jersey), and Paterson (New Jersey); a Roberto Clemente Middle School in Germantown (Maryland); and Roberto Clemente High Schools in Ann Arbor (Michigan) and Chicago.

New York State's highest honor is the Jackie Robinson Empire State Freedom Medal.

The Satchel Paige Elementary School is in Kansas City.

In connection with his 75th birthday, a New York waterway ferry was named for Yogi Berra. The ferry, a 79-foot catamaran, takes fans from Manhattan to a pier in the Bronx near Yankee Stadium.

Lakewood, Ohio, has named a Little League field for Jimmie Foxx, who lived in the Cleveland suburb after his retirement from baseball.

The George Wright Golf Club in Hyde Park, Massachusetts, is named for the Hall of Famer.

On April 4, 2000, Moreno Valley (California) High School named its baseball field after one of its graduates, Troy Percival.

The University of California, Irvine, Medical Center in Orange, California, recently renamed one of its rooms the Mo Vaughn Child Life Playroom in honor of the first baseman who donated money to the hospital when he was with the Angels.

Descendants and fans of J. Lee Richmond are raising funds to erect a historical marker to him at the Forest Cemetery in Toledo, Ohio, where he is buried. On June 12, 1880, pitching for Worcester, Richmond threw the first perfect game in major league baseball, beating Cleveland in the National League. He was also the first left-hander to win 20 games in a season and the first to win 30 (Worcester, 32 wins in 1880). Richmond died in 1929. A marker was placed at the field in Worcester to commemorate Richmond's perfect game.

The Bob Feller homestead at 29653 40th Terrace, Van Meter, Iowa, is listed on the National Register of Historic Places. Also on the register are Jackie Robinson's apartment (5224 Tilden Avenue, Brooklyn); Judy Johnson's house at 3701 Kiamensi Avenue, Wilmington, Delaware; Billy Sunday's house in the Winona Lake Historic District in Indiana; Jim Thorpe's house, 706 E. Boston Avenue, in Yale, Oklahoma; and William Wrigley Jr.'s "Winter Cottage," 2501 E. Telawa Trail, Phoenix, Arizona.

Yakima, Washington, is the site of Jason Stottlemyre Field, named for the son of Yankee pitcher and pitching coach Mel and brother of big league pitchers Todd and Mel Jr. Jason died of leukemia when he was 11.

The Arizona Diamondbacks have named their press lounge in honor of the late local television reporter Steve Pascente. Their press box is named for the late baseball writer Dick Dozer. His son Richard is president of the Diamondbacks.

San Francisco has renamed North Beach Playground after Joe DiMaggio over the objection of his lawyer. The plan had the approval of Joe's brother Dom. The DiMaggios grew up in San Francisco. The lawyer wanted the city to name a bridge or an airport for Joe D.

Q **Some ballplayers have baseball structures or strategies named after them—Greenberg Gardens, the Boudreau Shift, the Pesky Pole, the Mendoza Line, and so forth. One player had an entire era named for him. Who is he?**

Horace Clark, the pride of Frederiksted, Virgin Islands. An average player (.256 career bating average), Clark gave his name to the "Horace Clark Era" (1965–1974), a period of Yankee mediocrity when the team finished sixth, tenth, ninth, fifth, fifth, second, fourth, fourth, fourth, and second.

October 25, 1983, was proclaimed "Tippy Day" to honor Tippy Martinez in his hometown of La Junta, Colorado. A ballfield there was named in his honor.

Oroville, California, erected a sign which proclaimed it HOME OF GARY NOLAN.

The death of Aurelio Rodriguez galvanized the Hispanic community in Detroit, where he played from 1971 to 1979. Rodriguez died after being hit by a car as he was standing on a Detroit sidewalk signing autographs on September 21, 2000. A monument to Rodriguez is planned in the Mexican Town Community Cultural Center in southwest Detroit.

The Orioles donated $100,000 to create a park named for Hall of Famer Leon Day on the Trust for Public Land's Gwynnis Falls Trail in West Baltimore.

The City of Chicago has erected a historic marker at 4356 West Washington Boulevard honoring George Halas. He played in 12 games for the New York Yankees. "Papa Bear" was a pioneer in the National Football League as owner, coach, and executive of the Chicago Bears.

Another Chicago historic marker was erected to Hall of Famer Andrew "Rube" Foster. It stands at 39th and Wentworth, near the site of the original Comiskey Park.

The Colorado Rockies continue their laudable efforts to have their players donate money to construct youth baseball fields throughout Colorado—plus one in Cheyenne, Wyoming. The Mike Lansing T-Ball Complex in Westminster was the first in Colorado. 1999 saw the construction of the Girls Fast-Pitch Softball Field in Denver. So far, fields have been built by and named for Ellis Burks (2), Marvin Freeman, Dante Bichette (4), Walt Weiss (3), Larry Walker (5), Bill Swift (3), Darryl Kile, Andres Galarraga (3, including "Big Cat Field"), Kevin Ritz, Vinny Castilla (3), Jerry Dipoto (3), Eric Young, Denny Neagle, Kirt Manwaring (2), and Pedro Astacio (2). More are planned. Good.

Legendary Red Sox executive Lou Gorman told us that the baseball field at Stonehill College—his alma mater in Easton, Massachusetts—was named for him.

Oakland A's broadcaster Hank Greenwald and his wife, Carla, told us that they were married on May 17, 1970, the day Hank Aaron got his 3,000th hit. Their son Douglas Aaron was named for both Douglas MacArthur and Hank Aaron. Hank told us, "I was a great admirer of Aaron as a player and MacArthur as a historic figure. We figured Douglas Aaron were two names he could live with even if he had no interest in either." Douglas Aaron Greenwald is now the radio voice of the Fresno Grizzlies, the Giants' AAA farm club.

The City of South Miami, Florida, named a street "Andre Dawson Drive." He's a native of Miami.

A statue of Pee Wee Reese and his teammate Jackie Robinson will be erected at Keyspan Park—the Coney Island, New York, home of the Cyclones (Mets, Short Season Class "A").

The Pittsburgh Pirates unveiled a 12-foot-high bronze statue of their great Hall of Fame slugger Willie Stargell on April 7, 2001, the day their new PNC Park opened.

A sign outside the town of New Alouez, Michigan, proclaims it to be the "Home of George Brunet, Former Major League Pitcher."

In recognition of his contributions to the refurbishing of its baseball field, Phoenix House in Anaheim, California, named its baseball field for Gary DiSarcina.

Gallaudet University named its baseball field after William "Dummy" Hoy. Gallaudet, home of the Bisons, is a school for the hearing impaired in Washington, D.C., where Hoy, who became deaf at the age of two, broke into the majors with the Nationals in 1886.

There's an annual horse race at California's Hollywood Park in Inglewood called the "Jim Murray Memorial Handicap," named for the late Hall of Fame baseball writer.

A plaque honoring Carlton Fisk has been erected in Charlestown, New Hampshire, where he grew up. It's the first such plaque in New Hampshire to honor a living person.

Chuck Person, who played for the Indiana Pacers, Minnesota Timberwolves, San Antonio Spurs, Charlotte Hornets, and the Seattle Supersonics in the NBA, was named for Chuck Connors.

Connors' gravestone at Los Angeles's San Fernando Mission Cemetery includes the logos of his two big league teams, the Dodgers and the Cubs. Also included is the logo of the Boston Celtics, for whom he played briefly, and his likeness in his most famous role—Lucas McCain, *The Rifleman*. See www.seeingstars.com/ImagePages/ChuckConnorsGravePhoto.shtml.

Avon Park, Florida, renamed Castle Street, where Hal McRae used to play stickball, to "Hal McRae Boulevard."

Dave LaRoche named his son after Jeff Torborg, his manager with the Indians and the White Sox.

The St. Louis Cardinals will erect a statue to Hall of Famer James "Cool Papa" Bell. He started his career in 1922 with the St. Louis Stars in the Negro Leagues.

The Giants clubhouse at SBC Park was named the "Mike Murphy Clubhouse," after their equipment manager. Murphy has been with the Giants since they moved to San Francisco in 1958 and, through 1999, had never missed a Giants home game.

The luxury suites at Yankee Stadium are named for Dave Winfield, Reggie Jackson, Whitey Ford, Mickey Mantle, Lou Gehrig, Joe DiMaggio, Phil Rizzuto, Ron Guidry, Bill Dickey, Elston Howard, and Don Mattingly.

Miller Field's press box in Milwaukee is the "Bob Betts Press Box." Betts was the Brewers' public address announcer for 23 years. He died in 1999.

Baseball writers who have won the most prestigious award in baseball, the J. G. Taylor Spink Award—given at the Baseball Hall of Fame induction ceremonies—and broadcasters who have similarly been given the Ford C. Frick Award, have had their photographs mounted in the Angels Stadium press box dining room in Anaheim.

On October 6, 2001, the last game of the season and the last game of Cal Ripken Jr.'s legendary career, Baltimore named a street adjoining Camden Yards after him.

On September 25, 2001—the day of the Yankees' first home game after the September 11 attacks on the World Trade Center—the New York Yankees announced that they would erect, in Monument Park at Yankee Stadium, a monument to those who perished in the tragedy. The plaque was unveiled by Yankee legends Whitey Ford and Phil Rizzuto on September 11, 2002.

There's a "George Foster Home" for disadvantaged children in upper Dayton, Ohio.

New Rochelle, New York, has named a street after former resident Lou Gehrig.

El Paso's Cohen Stadium, home of the Diablos, was named for Andy and Syd Cohen, brothers who both played in the majors. Andy also managed the Phillies.

Si Rosenthal, who was Jewish, raised funds and donated funds himself for the creation of the Si Rosenthal Gymnasium at the Divine World Catholic Seminary in St. Louis, Missouri. Many of Rosenthal's plaques and awards are on display there.

Nolan Ryan's son Reese was named for Jimmie Reese, an Angels coach during Ryan's years there.

Manhattan's Carnegie Deli has named a sandwich after Mo Vaughn.

Rachel Prehodka-Spindel, an Atlanta Braves fan, has a parakeet named "Chirper Jones."
 Thanks to Dan Schlossberg for this item.

One of the most popular promotions in recent years has been the bobblehead doll giveaway night. But true bobblehead immortality has been achieved by only a few. During the 2002 season, these few players were honored by bobblehead giveaways from more than one team: Chipper Jones —Durham Bulls, Macon Braves, Richmond Braves, and Greenville Braves; Cal Ripken Jr. — Wilmington Blue Rocks, Frederick Keys, Delmarva Shorebirds, and Bowie Baysox; Mark McGwire —Modesto A's, Lansing Lugnuts; José Canseco—Modesto A's, Tacoma Rainiers.

Tommy John also achieved a sort of bobble immortality in 2002, when the Charlotte Knights gave away Tommy John bobble*arm* dolls (the head bobbles, too).

In 2003, the St. Paul Saints distributed bobblehead dolls in the likeness of St. Paul! In a full beard and two-tone toga, St. Paul is holding a Saints book in his left hand. He's leaning on a bat held in his right hand.

The Lowell (Massachusetts) Spinners issued Jack Kerouac bobblehead doll. Kerouac is a native of Lowell.

The Forth Worth Cats held an auction. The highest bidder (of 66) spent $5,200 on eBay to have the team produce and distribute 1,500 bobblehead dolls with his son's face on them.

The Camden River Sharks issued a bobblehead doll in the likeness of one of their interns for Intern Bobblehead Doll Night!

Arizona Diamondbacks and the United Blood Services gave away a special limited edition "Patriotic Diamondback Ubie" bobblehead doll to those who donated blood during critical times of the year. Quinton McCracken of the Diamondbacks encouraged donations during the week of September 11.

Starting in 2004, the top college pitcher will receive the "Roger Clemens Award."

There's a Jake Pitler Pediatric Playroom at Brooklyn's Beth-El Hospital.

"Curt Schilling Field" was dedicated on April 3, 2002, near Indian Bend Elementary School in Paradise Valley, Arizona. Schilling went to school there. The field is designed for Little League and features lights, a scoreboard, and a sprinkler system. It joins youth fields in and around Phoenix named for Randy Johnson, Jay Bell, Steve Finley, Brian Anderson, Todd Stottlemyre, Matt Williams, and Armando Reynoso.

On June 25, 2002, the Astros announced that they would erect a circular plaque at Minute Maid Field in Houston to Darryl Kile, who pitched for the Astros, 1991–1997.

Kile died four days before. The plaque will have Kile's initials, DK.

July 6, 2002, was Old Timers' Day at Yankee Stadium. It was also the day the Yankees unveiled a plaque to "Mr. October," Reggie Jackson.

The award to the most valuable player in the "Futures Game," played during the All-Star break, has been named for Hall of Famer Larry Doby. The winner will be awarded the Larry Doby Trophy, manufactured by Tiffany & Co.

The Philadelphia Phillies announced on June 5, 2002, that they had commissioned 10-foot-tall sculptures of four Phillies greats to be exhibited at their new ballpark. The four are Mike Schmidt, Richie Ashburn, Steve Carlton, and Robin Roberts.

WHO IS THE CHEESIEST BALLPLAYER AROUND? DEPARTMENT

No, not Jim, Johnny, Mike, or Tom Romano. The answer is John Kruk. As part of the 2002 Milwaukee, Wisconsin, All-Star Game "festivities," Kruk's likeness was rendered in 150 pounds of cheddar cheese as a promotion for his sports talk show.

Signs were erected in 2002 along South Carolina's routes US 521 and US 1 near Camden, South Carolina, proclaiming it to be BIRTHPLACE OF BASEBALL HALL OF FAMER LARRY DOBY.

On March 19, 2002, the Boston Red Sox official booster club, the BoSox Club, unveiled a plaque at the team's City of Palms spring training ballpark in Ft. Myers, Florida, to honor its first president, Dom DiMaggio.

Tommy Lasorda was on hand with about 500 others in Greenville, South Carolina, on July 14, 2002, for the dedication of a 450-pound bronze life-size statue of Shoeless Joe Jackson. Bricks from old Comiskey Park, where Jackson played with the White Sox, surround the statue's base.

Shortly after the July 17, 2002, death of their veteran trainer Jimmy Warfield, the Cleveland Indians announced that the Jacobs Field training room would be named in his honor. Warfield was with the Indians from 1971 to 2002. The Indians wore "JW" patches for the rest of the 2002 season.

The Homestead Hi-Level Bridge over the Monongahela River in Pennsylvania's Allegheny County was renamed the "Homestead Grays Bridge" on July 11, 2002. When the bridge is renovated by 2005, it will be decorated with banners with pictures of Grays players.

Great American Ballpark, new home of the Cincinnati Reds, features statues of memorable Reds Joe Nuxhall, Ernie Lombardi, Ted Kluszewski, and Frank Robinson.

The Atlanta Braves have announced that they will erect a statue of Warren Spahn outside Turner Field in Atlanta.

On August 11, 2002, the St. Louis Cardinals dedicated a statue to their newest Hall of Famer, Ozzie Smith, at Busch Stadium. Stan Musial, Lou Brock, Red Schoendienst, and Whitey Herzog were present for the ceremonies.

After 52 years with the Braves, trainer Dave Pursley retired after the 2002 season. In recognition of his devotion to the team and the players, the Braves renamed the trainer's room at Turner Field "Pursley's Place." The team also gave him a Lexus LS 450.

Danny Graves Field will be built, in cooperation with the Cincinnati Reds, in Cleves, Ohio. Graves has donated $5,000 for its creation.

The Cleveland Indians have named the radio announcer's booth of the visiting team at Jacobs Field after Ernie Harwell.

Thanks to the efforts of Evelyn Begley and Tom Gilbert of the Casey Stengel–New York chapter of the Society for American Baseball Research, a plaque will be mounted on the remaining wall of Washington Park, home of the Brooklyn Superbas/Dodgers from 1898 to 1912. The plaque will be accompanied by a photo and memorabilia exhibit and pamphlet showing the history of the park.

The Willie Mays Award for outstanding achievement in baseball is presented by the Profesional Baseball Scouts Foundation. The first recipient of the award was Willie Mays.

Shaun Clancy's new restaurant at 18 W. 33rd Street in New York City is called Foley's, named for veteran baseball writer Red Foley, author of *Ask Red*. Foley was at the grand opening on January 26, 2004.

The broadcast booth at SBC Park in San Francisco has been named the Hodges-Simmons Broadcast Center, for longtime Giants Hall of Fame broadcasters Russ Hodges and Lon Simmons.

Jim Thome has a street named after him in his native Peoria, Illinois.

Stewart Robert Thalblum, whose father, Mike, is the visiting clubhouse manager for the Oakland A's at Network Associates Coliseum, was named for Dave Stewart and Bob Welch.

Miguel Batista, who traces his ancestry to Caribe Indians, donated $50,000 for the construction of "Miguel Batista" field on the Gila River Indian reservation in Arizona. The field, the first built on tribal land funded by a player, has new fencing, an electronic scoreboard, a grass infield, dugouts, lighting, and an irrigation system.

The Dick Wantz Memorial trophy is given annually since 1966 by the Anaheim Angels to the player who shows the most dedication and improvement during minor league spring training camp. Wantz played for the Angels in 1965, pitching just one game. He died of a brain tumor a month later, at the age of 25.

Major League Baseball has declared April 15 to be Jackie Robinson Day. April 15 is the anniversary of the day Robinson broke baseball's color barrier with the Brooklyn Dodgers in 1947.

Harry K's, a restaurant built into the scoreboard in left field at the Phillies' new home, Citizens Bank Ballpark, is named for longtime voice of the Phillies, Harry Kalas. The restaurant is at the end of the park's entertainment zone called Ashburn's Alley, named for Philadelphia's favorite player and broadcaster, Richie Ashburn.

The Darryl Kile Award was established in 2002 by the Houston chapter of the Baseball Writers Association of America. It is given to the Astro who best reflects the decency and character of the late Astro pitcher.

COOPERSTOWN REPORT

Q **Only two Hall of Fame pitchers have hit grand slams and pitched no-hitters. Who are they?**
Walter Johnson and Bob Gibson.

Johnson pitched a no-hitter for the Washington Senators on July 1, 1920, against the Red Sox.

His grand slam came on June 21, 1914, off George Boehler in Detroit.

Bob Gibson pitched a no-hitter on August 14, 1971, and hit grand slams on September 29, 1965, off future Hall of Famer Gaylord Perry (in San Francisco) and again on July 26, 1973, off John Strohmayer of the Mets in St. Louis.

Q **Who is the only Hall of Famer to record a 20–20–20–20 season—20 doubles, 20 triples, 20 home runs, 20 stolen bases?**
Willie Mays, 1957 New York Giants: 26 doubles, 20 triples, 35 home runs, 38 stolen bases.

Q **Which switch-hitting Hall of Famer has driven in 100 runs in a single season in both leagues?**
Eddie Murray.

THIS IS NOT A TRICK QUESTION DEPARTMENT

Ted Williams hated the way his face appeared on his Hall of Fame plaque so much that he persuaded the Hall to redo it. Likewise, Bob Feller's original plaque showed that he played from 1936 to 1956. But between 1942 and 1944, he saw combat in the U.S. Navy, where he won eight battle stars. His plaque was redone to reflect his playing years lost to military service.

Q **Who is the only Hall of Famer whose *name* was changed on his plaque after his induction?**

Roberto Clemente. He was elected by acclamation by the Baseball Writers Association of America shortly after his death on New Year's Eve 1972, bringing relief supplies to earthquake-ravaged Managua, Nicaragua. Clemente's overloaded plane crashed into the sea shortly after takeoff from Puerto Rico. The five-year waiting period for induction was waived, and Clemente was inducted on August 6, 1973.

Clemente's name was originally written on his Hall of Fame plaque as "Roberto Walker Clemente." But his birth name was Roberto Clemente Walker. Twenty-seven years after his induction, the error was corrected, better to reflect his Hispanic heritage, and a new plaque was installed on December 16, 2000, as part of the hall's annual Holiday Festival.

Shortly after Carlton Fisk's induction on July 23, 2000, an error was discovered on his plaque. The plaque correctly notes that he caught more games than any other catcher but gave the wrong number of games: 2,229. The correct number is 2,226. The plaque was subsequently corrected.

THIS IS NOT A TRICK QUESTION DEPARTMENT

Q **Name three men who were inducted into the Hall of Fame in a hotel lobby.**

Duke Snider, Chuck Klein, and Al Kaline. They were inducted in the lobby of the historic and majestic Otesaga Hotel, overlooking Cooperstown's Lake Otsego in July 1980. It was raining, and the induction ceremonies had to be moved indoors.

Q **Name four men who lived long enough to say, "I was inducted into the Hall of Fame 40 years ago."**

Joe DiMaggio, Charlie Gehringer, Carl Hubbell, and Bob Feller.

DiMaggio was inducted in 1955 and died in 1999, 44 years later. Gehringer was inducted in 1949 and died in 1993, 44 years later. Carl Hubbell went into the hall in 1947 and died 41 years later, in 1988. Feller was inducted in 1962—and is still alive and well.

Q **Only one Hall of Famer has pitched and caught in the same game since 1900. Who is he?**

Roger Bresnahan, St. Louis Cardinals, August 3, 1910.

Q **Only one Hall of Fame pitcher gave up a home run to the first batter he ever faced in the majors. Who is he?**

Bob Gibson. On April 15, 1959, pitching in relief in his major league debut, the future Cardinal great (and future Mets "attitude coach") gave up a home run to Dodger third baseman Jim Baxes, leading off the seventh inning.

Coincidentally, Gibson also gave up a home run to the *last* batter he ever faced in the big leagues—Pete LaCock of the Cubs—a grand slam on September 13, 1975, the only grand slam of LaCock's career.

Talk about going out with a bang!

Q **Who was the first Hall of Famer to hit an extra-inning pinch-hit grand slam?**
Rogers Hornsby. On September 13, 1931, playing for the Cubs, Hornsby pinch-hit for Rollie Hemsley in the 11th inning and cleared the bases. The Cubs beat the Boston Braves 11–7.

Q **Which ballplayer had the most Hall of Fame teammates in his career (same team and year, though not necessarily in the same games)?**
It's a tie between Waite Hoyt and Burleigh Grimes: 36.

Q **Who is the only Hall of Famer to pinch-hit an inside-the-park grand slam?**
Hack Wilson, May 14, 1933. Wilson's Dodgers beat the Philadelphia Phillies at home 8–6.

Q **Nine of the men who pitched the first no-hitters for their teams wound up in the Hall of Fame. Who are they?**
Christy Mathewson threw the first no-hitter for the New York Giants, July 15, 1901.
Cy Young, Boston Red Sox, May 5, 1904 (a perfect game).
Walter Johnson, Washington Senators, July 1, 1920.
Jesse Haines, St. Louis Cardinals, July 17, 1924.
Hoyt Wilhelm, Baltimore Orioles, September 2, 1958.
Sandy Koufax, Los Angeles Dodgers, June 30, 1962.
Juan Marichal, San Francisco Giants, June 15, 1963.
Jim "Catfish" Hunter, Oakland Athletics, May 8, 1968 (a perfect game).
Phil Niekro, Atlanta Braves, August 7, 1973.

Q **Name two Hall of Famers who had gaps in their major league playing careers of at least 10 years.**
Satchel Paige. Although he "retired" in 1953, after a five-year major league career with the Cleveland Indians and St. Louis Browns, he made a triumphant if hokey return to the majors for one game with the 1965 Kansas City Athletics, a 12-year gap.

"Orator" Jim O'Rourke thought that his last game was in 1893. But he came back in 1904 for one game with the New York Giants—an 11-year gap.

Q **What's the connection: Hall of Famers Dan Brouthers, Carlton Fisk, Johnny Evers, Hughie Jennings, Ted Lyons, Phil Niekro, Jim O'Rourke, Satchel Paige, Nolan Ryan, Sam Thompson, and Hoyt Wilhelm.**
All played in the majors (a few as player-managers) after their 45th birthdays.

Q **Only one Hall of Famer had a game in which he hit three home runs *including two in the same inning*. Who is he?**
Hint #1: He did not hit 500 home runs in his career.
Hint #2: He did not hit 400 home runs in his career.
Al Kaline, Detroit Tigers, April 17, 1955 Kaline hit 399 career home runs.

Q **Ted Williams is well known for having served in both World War II and the Korean War. Only one Hall of Famer was in the military service (U.S. Army) in both World War I and World War II. Who is he?**
Larry MacPhail.

Q **Who are the only Hall of Famers to hit back-to-back inside-the-park home runs since 1900?**

Ty Cobb and Sam Crawford. They did it for the Detroit Tigers on August 27, 1909, in a game against the New York Highlanders.

Q **Which Hall of Famer hit grand slams for the most teams?**

Dave Winfield. He hit grand slams for five teams: Padres, Yankees, Angels, Blue Jays, Twins.

THIS IS NOT A TRICK QUESTION DEPARTMENT

Q **Who is the only man with two plaques displayed in the Hall of Fame?**

Roberto Clemente. His new, ethnically correct plaque is on display in the actual Hall of Fame Gallery. His first plaque (which, as noted, lists his name incorrectly as "Roberto Walker Clemente") is also on display at the Hall of Fame, in the children's room, adjacent to the library and the Bullpen Theater.

Q **Name a Hall of Famer who played in the All-Star Game for one league and in the World Series for the other league in the same year.**

Johnny Mize. In 1949, he was an All-Star with the Giants. After being acquired by the Yankees, he helped them win the World Series, beating the Brooklyn Dodgers 4–1.

Q **Only twice have Hall of Famers hit two grand slams in the same game. Who are they?**

Tony Lazzeri, New York Yankees, May 24, 1936.
Frank Robinson, Baltimore Orioles, June 26, 1970.

Q By 1998, with the birth of the Tampa Bay Devil Rays, each major league team has had a first designated hitter. Only one is a Hall of Famer. Who is he, and for which team did he play?

Orlando Cepeda, Boston Red Sox. He went 0 for 6 on April 6, 1973, against the New York Yankees.

Rickey Henderson of the San Diego Padres could join this very short list.

Q Only two Hall of Famers have hit three home runs in a game in both leagues. Which two?

Babe Ruth: New York Yankees, Boston Braves.

Johnny Mize: St. Louis Cardinals and New York Giants, New York Yankees.

Q What do Hall of Famers Gabby Hartnett, Joe Tinker, and Bucky Harris have in common?

They died on their birthdays.

Gabby Hartnett: born December 20, 1900; died December 20, 1972.

Joe Tinker: born July 27, 1880; died July 27, 1948.

Bucky Harris: born November 8, 1896; died November 8, 1977.

Q Only three Hall of Fame pitchers have recorded 100 wins and 100 saves in their careers. Which three?

Dennis Eckersley: 197 wins, 390 saves.

Hoyt Wilhelm: 143 wins, 227 saves.

Rollie Fingers: 114 wins, 341 saves.

Q **Home runs in the same inning by three Hall of Famers—a rare feat accomplished only seven times in history, including twice in 1932 and twice in 1934. This Hall of Famer was a part of a Hall of Fame–homering trio on four separate occasions. Who is he, and who were the others?**

Lou Gehrig, New York Yankees. On September 7, 1931, Babe Ruth, Gehrig, and Bill Dickey homered in the sixth inning of the second game of a doubleheader as the Yankees beat the Philadelphia Athletics 9–4.

On June 3, 1932, Gehrig, Ruth, and Earle Combs homered in the fifth inning. Yankees 20, Philadelphia A's 13. *What?! You scored 13 runs and still lost by 7?*

On May 28, 1934, Gehrig, Ruth, and Tony Lazzeri homered in the seventh inning in a 13–9 victory over the St. Louis Browns.

On August 2, 1934, Gehrig combined with Dickey and Lazzeri for three homers in the seventh inning, as the Yankees beat the Boston Red Sox 12–4.

About the Authors

Jeffrey Lyons is the entertainment critic for WNBC-TV in New York, the film critic for the NBC stations, and host of the nationally syndicated radio feature *The Lyons Den*. He has been a guest broadcaster for the Boston Red Sox in English and Spanish. His favorite players are Carl Yastrzemski and Wade Boggs.

Douglas B. Lyons, Jeffrey's younger brother, is a criminal lawyer in New York City. His favorite players are Willie Mays and Dave Winfield.

They have collaborated on *Out of Left Field* and *Curveballs and Screwballs*. Douglas B. Lyons is also the coauthor of *Broadcast Rites and Sites—I Saw It on the Radio with the Boston Red Sox* (with Joe Castiglione) and *From an Orphan to a King* (with Eddie and Anne Marie Feigner).